Martin Leidenfrost
INTIMATE BRUSSELS

Martin Leidenfrost
INTIMATE BRUSSELS
Living amongst Eurocrats

Translated from the German
by Carolina Stiberg

Edition**Andreae**

Martin Leidenfrost, born 1972 in Lower Austria, writes books, essays, screenplays and columns. His central-European stories in "The World beyond Vienna" (2008) were awarded with the international journalism prize "Writing for CEE 2007". Leidenfrost lives and works in Devínska Nová Ves, at the Slovak-Austrian border river Morava.

All rights reserved. No part of this publication may be reproduced, stored in a retrieval system, or transmitted in any form by any means, electronic, mechanical, photocopying, recording or otherwise, without prior written permission of the publisher.

The publisher expressly disclaims all responsibility and liability with regard to the topicality, correctness, completeness or quality of the information provided.

Original title: Brüssel zartherb. Fünfzig europäische Expeditionen
Originally published in Austria by: Picus Verlag Ges.m.b.H., Vienna
© 2010 Picus Verlag Ges.m.b.H., Vienna

English Translation
© 2011 Lexxion Publisher, Berlin
www.lexxion.eu

ISBN Print: 978-3-86965-156-9
ISBN E-Book: 978-3-86965-157-6

Editor: Bettina de Keijzer
Cover Picture: © Martina Hartl
Design and Typeset: Annika Langer, Berlin
Printer: fgb freiburger graphische betriebe, Freiburg/Brsg.

Contents

Introduction	7
The Arrival	13
The Couchsurfers	16
On the Bus	23
In Love, Almost	26
Gotham City	31
The Parliament	35
The Council	40
Coffee House Feature	45
The Fat	49
At the Meat Market	54
The Centre	63
The Albanians	67
The Portuguese	71
The Finns	74
The Civil Servants	78
The Sceptics	83
Chat by the Fire with the Congolese	88
Studio Europe	94
Nocturne	98
The Rocco Case	101

The Hunters	108
The Directory	112
Lost Sectors	117
The Security	121
The Tobacco Lobby	125
Facebook	129
The Fire	133
Why Sliven?	138
In the Container	142
The Beds	147
The Hans-Gert-Machine	155
That's Why Sliven	159
The Ditches	167
The Murder Ballad of Section Z	171
The Raid	174
The African Commission	177
The Muslims	181
The Children	184
The Chinese	187
The Churches	191
The Christians	195
The Italians	199
The Soviet Union	203
The Llamas and the Fat Cats	207
The Boredom	212
The Refuge	216
On Holiday	220
Final Remark	224
Sex and the Valley	233

Introduction

Once, back in the 1990's, I unexpectedly made a group of young women dream. I was myself young at the time, rather depressed, slept a lot, hardly ever left the house and pondered much over thoughts of no real importance, at least not outside the four walls of my room. Having nonetheless quite surprisingly ended up amongst people, that young depressed boy tried one of his useless thoughts on a group of young Austrian girls.

This particular thought – the transformation of the European Union into a constitutional empire – was rather half-baked. I wasn't held back by the problem of the majority of the Member States being republics. Offhandedly, I coupled the attractive offspring of two European royal families; Princess Diana's blond son William and the brunette Swedish Princess Victoria, and then described the inconceivably dignified railway carriage in which the Prince of Wales travels every so often through the luscious green English landscape. In such a wagon, I persisted, our beautiful imperial couple would roll through all of Europe. My vision was inspired by the spirit of the magazines that you find in the waiting room at the dentist's. The girls at the table were by no means royalists, one of them ended up with a French Trotskyite, but that night her eyes were sparkling. Our conversation rose into a proper imperial frenzy.

I mention these moments, which are lost upon world history, since I can't remember seeing a single person dream of the European institutions. It got around that by now more than seventy percent of the national legislation is being negotiated at EU level. However, nowhere else can the sphere of the dreamlike, the nightmarish intertwining and fantasy-filled thrills be less expected than there.

Later, after my depression had come to an end, I left my room and wrote screenplays for movies and TV. I loved watching the TV-series "Sex and the City", and from this show an idea arose. The four New York thirty-something heroines were excellent. But couldn't such sharp-minded characters be found in Europe as well? And couldn't the European Carries, Mirandas, Charlottes and Samanthas be found right there in the capital of Europe? Couldn't the incessantly bubbling battlefield that is the singles' world be enriched by the relationships, emotions, romances and spitefulness existing between the dozens of nations in Europe? I was convinced that the TV-audience would thank and reward me for such a series. However, as expected, I didn't pursue the idea any further. I didn't even write a concept. What I was lacking was expertise; I had never even been to Brussels.

Even later, I was already approaching thirty and an unsettling craving to explore the eastern European Slavic countries hit me. Dozens of times, I roamed the country which attracted and confused me the most, the Ukraine. In 2004, at the same time as the eastern expansion of the European Union, I finally moved eastwards. It was only a slight eastbound move, from Vienna to the Slovakian shores of the border river Morava, yet in doing so I finally became notorious as a proper Eastern bod. From my Slovakian point of observation I wrote a column about "The World beyond Vienna". Since I was now living at the very seam of the Iron Curtain describing a multi-ethnic area marked by borders, I could conclude the following: I was unconditionally telling a story about Europe.

The previously mentioned ideas merged together in my head. The reactions of my friends and readers ranged from surprise to shock, but to me it seemed like the only logical next step: someone like me needed to write a column from Brussels. Had my fellow "Easterners" not all moved to that very capital by now? Wouldn't they, at least the females, like to rough up this saturated western cadre? Wasn't Carrie Bradshaw, the main character in "Sex and the City", a columnist? Didn't she publish a weekly column about sex in the metropolis? Was I not a columnist myself?

With these unsorted thoughts I started promoting myself. In Vienna, I sat down with the head of department of the finest weekend supplement in Austria and his editor in chief. I told them I wanted to write something like "Sex and the City" from Brussels, only with less sex and more Europe. The editor looked at me, slightly amused and slightly shocked. My proposition was accepted.

I still didn't go to Brussels. My intention was to go there with an open and almost naïve mind, ready for anything, with a stranger's view on things. For a year I prepared myself, compiling an extensive archive of stories, statistics and peculiarities from all European nations.

I made myself familiar with the topic of my future column. At least fifty thousand people in Brussels are defining regulations for five hundred million people. That was my starting point. Some people argued that there were one hundred thousand. I began to totalise. Of the twenty-five thousand European Commission officials, eighteen thousand were working in Brussels. Added to this, three thousand two hundred European Council members, a little over three thousand employees of the European Parliament in Brussels, another thousand in the Committee of the Regions and in the European Economic and Social Committee, as well as temporary employees in the European institutions. Two thousand seven hundred free-lancing interpreters, one thousand four hundred accredited journalists; eight hundred of them living permanently in the city. Seven hundred and fifty European delegates, twice as many assistants. One thousand "Securitas" guards assigned by the European institutions and some more from competitive firms. Several thousand interns present at any time. Thousands of employees working for permanent representations to the EU and the regional offices. The personnel in the off-site cafeterias, the catering business and in cleaning service were a bit harder to approximate. And in addition to the Commission officials, the impressive single army of maybe fifteen thousand lobbyists. I didn't include relatives and experts flying in day after day. The calculation added up to a sum of about sixty thousand people who refine Europe every workday.

I had to convince more European newspapers to take on my column. I wrote to them: "We don't know these people, the European Union doesn't have any myths, and its central characters don't have faces. What if someone took a look at these people? If he strolled through Brussels, down side-paths and through back doors, studying fairies and brownies in that European bubble? If he descended to their dealers, prostitutes and cleaners, mingled with their Belgian, Arabic or African neighbours, if he observed and described their styles, their affairs and their forms of expression?"

Little by little more newspapers got on board, two from Switzerland, two from Germany and one from Slovakia. Eventually, single pieces were translated into English, French, Ukrainian and Bulgarian. Truthfully, I had written to the newspapers: "I don't know what to expect. If I find Gomorrah, I will write about it. If I find tribal feuds or completely sterile Europeans, then I will write about that. And if I find boredom, then it is boredom I will write about." However, I had also given the quite reckless promise that I would portray all European nations through the prism of the European bubble that is Brussels.

I still didn't know Brussels. When I took off for the city, I really felt like a European Carrie Bradshaw. Except that I had chosen a place that was, at best, known by collective ignorance. That I had chosen the abominable governess who constantly alerts from afar: don't smoke, don't form monopolies, don't discriminate! That my choice had fallen upon a place, at which even the most sympathetic friend would roll his eyes. "Good luck!" I would hear more than once, "it's the most boring city in the world".

The Arrival

Almost everyone in Brussels is a stranger. The European visitors are strangers to one another. The visitors to the Belgians, the Belgians to the visitors and even the Belgians – the Flemings and the Walloons – to themselves.

Perhaps it's so easy to get on board here since being estranged is normal. Now let me make note of the arrival, the first impression, the first pictures. Otherwise they may be forgotten by tomorrow, maybe I would be but a memory by tomorrow.

First: the airport. It greets me with the greasiness of an old salesman. A fifteen minute hasty trot is the designated time frame to the luggage hall, over moving walkways into a narrow shopping mall, upstairs, downstairs, through several winding chicanes, where I ask myself worriedly: "Am I lost?" Finally, at the luggage retrieval, there is an announcement: "The Brussels Airport advises you to take official taxis only." Afterwards an overbearing song played on full volume; "My Way" in French.

Secondly: the European Quarter. See above, the sense of airport lingers. In every building of the European institutions I'm screened. Again I take off my blazer; again I put it in a blue box. The sensors are set to a tolerable level, they don't react to belt buckles.

They don't react to cuff links either, and these are quite important. Nowhere better than in London Town, had I seen such a formal standard, especially of men's clothing. In the season of 08/09, the young Eurocrat wears a dark blue suit, a light blue shirt and a dark blue tie; which is the preferred choice of clothing of the current President of the European Council, Nicolas Sarkozy. Ties are all plain, hardly loosened by anyone. Suddenly I feel naked without my cuff links.

Thirdly: the city. Friendly admonitions are emblazoned on the facades of the European institutions; on the Parliament building it reads "take care, not antibiotics", on the Commission "road-safety in our cities", with a giant picture of a green traffic light sporting a big grin.

Inside the buildings, the European visitors lead a life of short intense briefings. When a briefer takes his time, he announces a "sixty-minute-briefing", which is perceived as unusually long. Commissioners never brief longer than twenty or thirty minutes.

Visitors constantly say the same things about the city. "Always this drizzle", "they cannot even build a proper pavement", "you would think differently of the capital of Europe". The snappy ones maintain that the drinking water contains more pollutants than the water in Bangladesh and that the Brussels Métro was really planned for Kinshasa. I don't know how to respond. I love taking a stroll on the slightly bumpy pavements outside the European Quarter. The whining about the Belgian climate I initially consider a bit of an exaggeration. Upon my arrival in September, Brussels is blessed with a beautiful Indian summer.

Fourthly: where second and third meet. One ordinary morning in the café "Chez Bernard", not far from the European institutions. Outside, Eurocrats are biking to work wearing full armour of shirts and suits, many even wearing yellow safety vests. Inside, a couple of true Belgians.

A small woman comes in, about forty, the southern European type. I don't notice her at first, but then she opens her trolley case at the leg of the bar stool, it's one of those ubiquitous hard-shelled ones, hand luggage compliant, and in the course of a few seconds she has gone through a routine with perfect military precision.

She jumps out of her black, conservative stiletto shoes and slips into a similar beige model. She takes out a travel laptop, puts it on the trolley's pulling handle, throws the black shoes in and closes it. Earlier her shoes went with her black vest, now with her beige shirt. She downs an espresso and takes off, with a half-smoked cigarette in her hand.

The old Belgians, smoking and reading, don't look up. They've seen it all before. Heading back home now, to look for my cuff links. Next time, I'll be part of it.

The Couchsurfers

A few days before my first departure I became anxious because I still didn't know where to stay in Brussels. Granted, I had decided not to take any fixed accommodation and instead just roam the city and explore its everyday life like a nomad. However, now I had nothing at all. I had to do something.

I wrote to unknown friends of friends. I posted an appeal in the *Yahoo* group for German-speaking Brussels interns, a thousand members in size. That didn't help much. Eventually I joined a community, which at that point already had seven hundred thousand members: *www.couchsurfing.com*.

I can say, couchsurfing worked. An intense tour through the unknown city awaited me, a real relay race of international solidarity. When couchsurfing ceased to work, there was a Brussels laundrette at my disposal, in all of its charming glory of intimacy.

Couchsurfing is an Internet community for travel-happy contemporaries, who let strangers stay the night, for free and for a short while. A safety problem is lurking behind this, which is why the predominantly American network presents a complex system of mutual guarantees. Guests and hosts evaluate each other through references, friendship is established through seven quality steps, and above the rank and file there is a thoroughly tested elite of "verified members".

Shortly after I had put my profile online I received a message from America. A leading member politely asked me to improve my laboriously completed profile according to the standard model and reveal more about myself. I have fallen victim to a sect, I thought, and took off on my journey feeling eminently sceptical.

My first host picked me up at the Brussels airport. On the dashboard of his small off-roader he had placed a nodding plastic Jesus and a Virgin Mary from Colombia. When I asked him about them, he immediately assured me that he was indeed Polish but by no means a Catholic fundamentalist. I was never really worried about that since the avowed Eurocrat was *verified* in other exemplary ways as well. He had a profession which "only existed in the EU" and which only in the EU seven hundred specialists practise: linguist lawyer. In addition to his ten languages, the man in his mid-thirties was currently learning Romanian. Thanks to her Polish passport, his wife, a smart and sensitive Brazilian of Japanese descent, was also allowed to work for the EU. She was involved in the NGO "World Vision", being a sponsor for two kids from Bolivia and Senegal whom she didn't know personally.

The bunk bed in the kids' room was empty; I slept there. My hosts took care of me unobtrusively, we had stimulating conversations and after two days I moved on from the bourgeois Stokkel to the borders of the African neighbourhood.

Since the couchsurfer is obliged to bring his own bedding, my luggage was very heavy. Dragging my giant suitcase behind me, I experienced the city in a unique way. At times I thought to myself: if you didn't see a Belgian every now and then, you would think that Brussels had been built for Pygmies. Since I was fretting to scuff my knees at the knees of my fellow human beings, I didn't sit in the Métro's four-seat compartment at first. Then there were the houses, often only two windows wide, the narrow staircases. I noticed a laundrette every hundred metres. Of course, I told myself straight away, I would rather die than try hauling a washing machine into one of these little dollhouses.

I stayed two days on the outskirts of the African neighbourhood, on the couch of an American-Flemish couple. They were extreme bikers and extreme hikers and extremely focused on their ecological footprint. The husband was from New York; he fought with subsiding confidence for the publication of his short stories, and was presumably secretly jealous of my glamourous Carrie-Bradshaw-project. Between his Flemish wife and me, an unspoken dislike slowly arose. In real life we would have stayed out of each other's way, now I slept on the sofa in their small living room; that, too, is couchsurfing.

Couchsurfing equals socialising. Your hosts introduce you to their friends and take you to other hosts and couchsurfers. My most unforgettable encounter was with an Asian female couchsurfer from San Francisco. She had made her trip to Europe possible by working as a stripper. She told me, that one of the regular customers at her peep show was from Japan. The Japanese gentleman always showed up with his sex painted red and on his red-painted sex glitter was sparkling. Once she had asked him for an explanation. The regular explained that his sexuality was repressed in Japan. He said, this way he wanted to re-establish esteem for his gender.

If not real mates, the couchsurfer does still make many "friends". "Cheap friends", as the young timid Romanian Liliana put it, who allowed me to stay on a mattress in her Franco-Belgian stoner student flat-share. The characteristic references couchsurfers constantly attribute to each other turned out to be absolutely true. They were all "open-minded", and "partying" with them was indeed "fun".

The fact that I didn't really feel at ease amongst couchsurfers probably transpires through my story. Though I should thank all of them, because after my two weeks as a couchsurfer, my circle of Brusselian acquaintances was fairly complete. There was the tall Romanian Liliana, who always pulled up her shoulders while walking, which maybe could explain her timid look. She was clever, multilingual and intellectual, worked for a French Helium corporation and was really bored in Brussels. She took an active interest in my project. Then there was a certain Polish guy.

He didn't really have anything to do with couchsurfing, he had just been sent to me as a one-off going out stand in. They couldn't have sent me a better guy than Staszek.

Like I said, couchsurfing had been working really well. A female reporter occasionally left her attic to me and at weekends, when the hotel prices in this city of conferences would fall considerably, I recovered in hotels. I was convinced that couchsurfing was the easiest thing in the world. Then came my last stop. Then came Brusselian sleeping place number 7, the south-European artist's quarter Saint Gilles, the Belgian artist Alessia. Alessia was the only local that I had managed to scrape up in the Brussels section of couchsurfing. But Alessia wasn't at home.

It was eight o'clock, dark, the alley was quiet. A narrow house, its windows dark. Four bells; I rang Alessia's. On the second floor a window was open, I could hear the bell ring from inside. I hadn't been able to reach Alessia earlier so I tried again. A voicemail advised me to call back later.

The open window instilled some hope in me. Was the fair artiste asleep? I crossed the street, waited until some people had passed and called out: "Alessiaaa!" I called out again, slowly and stretched out with the kind of melancholy of a serenading lover scorned. No one appeared in the open window.

I left to wait in a café. There wasn't any, only a laundrette on Chaussée de Waterloo. I rolled my suitcase inside and sat down in a plastic armchair overlooking the long row of washing machines. Five out of thirteen washing machines were turning. At first I was embarrassed, yet I realised quickly that nothing seems more natural to people than someone waiting in a laundrette.

"Bonsoir!" a tall African greeted me, as he came in with his wife to give her a hand with the dryers in the back. Many of the few laundrette visitors were wearing slippers. A big basket was moved, a giant IKEA-bag was filled, my suitcase fit nicely into the picture. I started to feel at ease. There was a machine that changed notes into coins, one selling drinks on the top and laundry detergent at the bottom and a coffee machine. The radio played carefully chosen chansons.

Several times a small woman in her forties came in wearing soft golden shoes. The only one staying throughout the whole washing cycle was a tall man in his fifties, actually looking respectable, yet lost, almost ashamed, lingering by the entrance. He reeked of alcohol. I forced myself to read, a poem by Heidegger, but I couldn't get past the one verse: "Armutbereite Stätte sterblichen Wohnens." – "Places of mortal dwelling primed for poverty." With that, hadn't everything been said?

Suddenly I noticed a white postbox hanging on the wall behind me with a piece of cloth sticking out. I pulled on it, some black sexy lingerie fell out. Guiltily, I looked around me. No one had seen it happen. I put the panties back in the postbox. On the box it said: "Suggestions".

Around nine o'clock I went back to Alessia's. I rang the doorbell, called out her name, nothing. I realised to my astonished joy that I could return to the laundrette. It closed at ten.

Only one machine was turning still, the woman with the golden shoes was letting her younger partner fold the laundry. Little by little I understood that the young Arab in slippers who was cleaning the machines was actually working there. He noticed me and smiled at me inquiringly. I didn't dare explain the concept of couchsurfing in French so I gave him a rough summary of the situation: had a rendezvous, woman didn't show up, have to wait, since I have to stay at the woman's place. "When was this rendezvous supposed to happen?" he asked smilingly. "At eight", I replied. He laughed and sympathetically allowed me to wait in the laundrette. The panties were gone.

Alessia wasn't around at ten either. I stayed in a hotel. The following night Alessia was at home. She took me in and she was nice to me. The mobile network operator was to blame, which in any case is the true nemesis of European integration. There is a lot to improve, that's for sure, but not in the laundrette in Chaussée de Waterloo. No, no suggestions. It's all good, good night.

On the Bus

In dark December, I happened to find myself travelling by coach on two consecutive occasions. The first one was an overnight drive of 16 hours straight through Europe, amidst travellers predominantly with darker skin tone. The other was a day excursion, with German Eurocrats. That sounds like a cheap comparison. However, I incidentally spent the same amount of time with both groups.

The night journey, operated by Eurolines, took me from Bratislava to Brussels. To sum it up: brrr! I got on board in the dark, at six o'clock. The journey ran from early dusk in the east to late dawn in the west. We drifted deeper and deeper into the damp, foggy winter night.

Nobody switched on the reading lights. On the bus there were Slovakian Roma, lone travellers from far away, two Indians, and probably a few migrant workers. In front of me sat a hooded couple in silence; he was Slovakian, she Russian from Kazakhstan.

In Vienna, a young blonde got on the bus. She took a seat behind me. She brought a lot of cute bags with her as well as a faint scent of cinnamon. I was convinced that the doll-faced beauty had rounded off her Christmas shopping with mulled wine.

The night got quieter. I couldn't fall asleep and engaged the blonde in conversation. She was Hungarian. She had the same name as the last Austro-Hungarian empress, only with an o. Zito was a beautician, 31 years old and her cinnamon scent was due to her use of essential oils.

She spoke German with a specific cadence to her Hungarian accent and answered "wow!" to most of what I said. She had been living in Brussels for seven years – "seven meagre years". Despite Hungary's "collapse", as she called it, she had returned to Budapest. We soon touched upon the more important issues. It was over with her French boyfriend. Completely unabashed, she declared that a new man would indeed come in handy.

The bus stopped in front of an Austrian roadside restaurant. We sat down at the bar, glancing nervously at the clock. I mentioned that we happened to be in the area where I grew up. "So if we were to miss the bus", Zito said, "would that be a sign from God?" "You mean", I replied, "that I could then introduce you to my mum straight away?" Her freshly made-up lips formed a smile and her knee gently stroked my leg.

Back in the dark bus, it got even colder. The others were prepared; Zito had a blanket with her. "Cover yourself with your coat!" she said and gave me her kidney-shaped travel cushion. We slept; the great land of Germany was dark. Zito's cushion helped me get through the night.

The day excursion, operated by the "Europa-Union", went from Brussels into the eastern Belgian provinces. Zito hadn't known that the EU employed Commissioners, but my new fellow travellers knew that only too well. They worked for the Commission and German representations in Brussels. One was an intern at the lobby for district heating. "Why does district heating need a lobby?" I asked her. "Well, to begin with, to let people know that there is such a thing as district heating."

The cheerful tour guide handed out gingerbread on several occasions, but the atmosphere wasn't all that convivial. People spoke about flight connections and about the fact that the Lisbon Treaty wasn't suitable for plebiscites.

Coincidentally, there was another Hungarian blonde on the bus, however she spoke completely accent-free German. As the conversation turned to Christmas presents, she let slip that "women are happy about any gift anyway". The others reacted astonished. She blushed. That was the most intimate moment we shared.

Well, it is a cheap comparison. German bureaucrats are perhaps just as gentle at night. I didn't ask Zito for her number and I didn't give the other Hungarian woman a present. But I take my hat off to all the bus-travelling Hungarian girls in this world.

In Love, Almost

Sometimes I feel like declaring my love for Brussels. If I were to direct this noblest of human emotions at a territory, then there would only be room in my heart for Brussels as a second runner up. My utmost affection, albeit foolish, delirious and passionate, will always be for the Ukraine. The second, which is more of a marriage-like commitment, I have with the central European open space between the Alps and the Carpathians, the world beyond Vienna. What would Brussels be then? Brussels would perhaps be a somewhat dingy mistress discovered in later years, but whom you would protect against bad-mouthing.

In any case, I discovered that I had started to defend the city against allegations. The Eurocrats raise all kinds of discontents towards their capital; they're united especially in their contempt for the Brusselian pavements. But once I found the defence rather bitter. I had to defend Brussels to the only Eurocrat that I had befriended in Brussels.

Regarding Staszek, first I have to mention how happy I am that he exists. The EU civil servant was always ready to go out, he had not found a woman after four and a half years in Brussels. That almost put women in a bad light, since the 33-year old was smart and funny, spoke seven languages and, before he totalled his mini-car, he carried his wish to integrate so far that he would listen to Flemish radio while driving at night, actually making out the differences between the Flemish dialects. Staszek looked like a normal guy, pleasant, slightly chubby and reliable, just like a Pole, a Pole with his heart in the right place. He came from the pious Polish foothills of the Carpathians. He didn't fit in with the Brussels lifestyle, he suffered like a dog in the European Quarter, and his homosexual to metrosexual to asexual colleagues all gave him a hard row to hoe. He named himself the last of the Mohicans.

With Staszek I could go all out. After seeing a shop that had an offer for "plasticisation", we applied that to the breed of people of the European institutions. "They are plasticised", I shouted, "and they want to plasticise us all." – "Exactly", Staszek shouted back, "the EU is the new Soviet Union."

The estrangement was unexpected. I was walking with Staszek on a traditional Brusselian pavement when he suddenly called it dirty and bad. He expressed himself exactly as these plasticisers would. "Et tu, Brute!" crossed my mind. Staszek, you who verify Polish translations with legal terminology on workdays, do you also share that same normative, levelling and harmonising view?

I wouldn't have known so much about the Brusselian pavements, hadn't it been for the unpredictability of the buses and trams. The bus is either stuck or throws you off halfway through the route; the tram spontaneously changes destination; one rainy night, an Arab holding a rose and I were carried in the wrong direction but the driver ignored our cries. In no other city do I walk as much.

I don't defend the city because of it being a functioning community, but because of its cosy shabbiness and its bourgeois grandeur that put together seem lovable to me. I enjoy being called "Monsieur"; I have always wanted to be a Monsieur. The little bakeries keep their bread on beautiful wooden shelves, and in the patisseries with all the fine cakes and pastries, conversations are held just like at the jeweller's.

From winter strolls, I keep a picture in my mind, looking into the broad windows of numerous restaurants with dimmed lights and seeing thin, dark-haired Mademoiselles sitting at small tables for two, wearing smooth fitting cashmere on their upright bodies. In this exquisite candlelight gallery, anyone would look like they were out on a date.

I also learned to appreciate the opposite, a hundred smoky beer joints, always under the same oldish beer brand "Jupiler Taverne". And the dirty white containers where a Monsieur – "une grande frite, s'il vous plait!" – can be served the tastiest chips in this galaxy.

My spontaneous affection had a lot to do with Alessia. The 31-year old disaster woman, more bartender than artist, introduced me to another Brussels just in time. Such things as briefings didn't exist in this world; every drink was followed by another, and with Alessia one could easily plummet into first class ruin. She found Eurocrats simply boring and arrogant. You couldn't blame the fanatic Brusselian for that. Which city would without further ado bear the landing of sixty thousand Martians, who earn twice or even three times as much as the locals, and who, rolling their eyes, call their landing place "the Balkans of the West".

Alessia didn't mess around with Eurocrats though; she had devoted herself entirely to her sex life. She broke up with her boyfriend and her lover, to subsequently return to them, to boyfriend and lover alike. All her men stood out due to their very non-Belgian passionate tempers. Once, one lover cut off the tie of another. Alessia could explain that very well: "He was just jealous; he's got both Breton and Corsican blood in him."

Always short on cash, Alessia constantly talked about wanting to settle down and focus on her art in peace. At one point, she welcomed me in a fluster, while jumping around on scattered pieces of clothing. She had worked out how many men she had slept with throughout her life and was now, adding on a few women, at a number over fifty. She shook her curly hair in horror and shouted: "That's too many, that's too many!"

She lived close to a prison. When she walked past there on summer nights and the cell windows were open, the prisoners would hear her heels click against the pavement.

At times, a prisoner would cry out vows of love into the night. Alessia found that quite erotic. When she learned that a friend was released from prison and at home with an electronic ankle monitor, she just had to visit him. She had to know what sex involving electronic ankle monitors felt like. And she found out.

The giant art poster under which I had first slept in Alessia's flat contained everything that a declaration of love for Brussels needed: eyes closed, a curly-haired brunette wearing a red dress was lying on cooled lava. Above it read in big letters the most poetic of all Flemish words: "Baraque Frituur" – "chip shop".

All this I should have told the lonely Eurocrat Staszek when he scolded the Brusselian pavements in a familiar tone. Instead I took a loose stone from the pavement. "Under the paving stones, the beach" was a slogan from the past. The stone was heavy, the beach in this case moist black dirt.

I told Staszek that at least it was a real pavement; at least it was suitable for a revolution. He grimaced. And I thought: if it were up to these Eurocrats, where would they have built the capital of Europe? I prefer not to know the answer.

Gotham City

I was asleep, in the back seat of a car, on a Belgian highway. As previously arranged I was dropped off in Brussels, at the Schuman roundabout, in the midst of the European institutions. It was dark. Drowsily I looked around me. The neighbourhood was deserted.

I took off, towards the hotel. No one, anywhere, only the noise from the through traffic. A young Oriental man rushed in the opposite direction, dressed in a white full-length robe, singing in Arabic. Soon I was alone again. Still not fully awake, suddenly the whole unleashed Orient was coming towards me. Men dressed in traditional robes, veiled mothers, one determined movement. Thousands of Muslims surged this night towards the Métro stop Schuman, which is the aorta of European businesses on workdays. I don't mean for it to be symbolic. That's just how it was.

At least once I wanted to have wandered through the European quarter at night. The inhumane street canyons in the comic fantasy "Gotham City", I imagined, could be perfectly actualised on a couple of square kilometres of Brussels.

On a Saturday night I returned, again in the dark, again at ten o'clock. Again I started at Schuman, however this time I didn't come across any Muslim, the "Great Mosque" in "Jubelpark" was silent.

I went up avenue de Cortenbergh, impressive office buildings and picturesque residential side streets. Cortenbergh was a disappointment to me, since I met someone every five minutes. I strolled back to Schuman.

The headquarters of the European Commission was tolerable to look at, scattered dim lights shining in the bend of the curved construction. Across the street "Justus Lipsius" was squatting, the broad colossus of the European Council, venue of governmental and ministerial top meetings and first legislator of the European Union. Three wings spread out on 215,000 square metres, with the appearance of a district health insurance office gone insane, a massive barrier in the centre of the European quarters. Only in the solitude of the night did the piece of art on the construction catch my attention, an illustration of that Phoenician princess that strictly speaking wasn't European, a metallic Europe. Anorexic, with the bust of an Amazon and wiry witch's hair, she was sitting upon a scrawny horse caught in a leap.

I went down rue de la Loi, preferable to Cortenbergh. A straight passage route with four lanes, filled with noisy waves of traffic. In the side streets nothing but empty office spaces. Taking note of all people passing by was not hard work. Between the unlit administration blocks one house struck me that had eluded me during the day. One last classic two-storey building, thinly forged iron bars in front of its glass entrance door. Gently illuminated from the inside a fine cross was traced on the glass, surrounded by a circle. It said: "Church of Scientology International. European Office for Public Affairs & Human Rights".

I went down rue Belliard. I had arrived, Gotham City at its best, inimitable. A racing track, five lanes, where traffic was speeding like bullets at one hundred kilometres per hour into the open mouth of a tunnel. Unlit office castles, most of them eight storeys high, some without a single reference to their occupants. I could pick out the Commission building DIGIT, the Lithuanian and Baden-Württemberg representations. The pavement was narrow and dark. In the airstream of passing cars I asked myself: after hours, were these thousands of officials thrown at the seventh gate of hell?

I have never found a purer emptiness, anywhere. Even in the quiet side streets, passing office building after office building, I was alone.

After three hours I walked down to the bottom of the valley, generally known as "Vallée des Eurocrates" – "Valley of the Eurocrats". On one side, the brown and gloomy Council colossus "Justus Lipsius" was cowering. On the other side, the valley led all the way up to the European Parliament, through Parc Léopold.

At the bottom was a concrete-covered park with twenty-four fountains. I had never seen anyone there, not even during the day. There were forty-eight park benches for forty-eight absent loving couples. I took a break on one of them.

My gaze fell on the fountains and I paused. The water from the fountains facing the Council building was gushing, as it should, one metre high, slightly curved from the whiffs of wind. The fountains facing the Parliament, however, were only squirting out fist-sized sprays from the concrete base, the drain was blocked, the fountains were choking on their own excess water.

I don't mean for it to be symbolic. As if the European Parliament – that should not be allowed to call itself a Parliament according to the doctrines of democratic separation of powers – would choke on its own statements. That's just how it was.

The Parliament

It can only be explained by this house, that even I, though rather tough, was almost brought to tears a couple of times. This house; the European Parliament building in Brussels. I'm not talking about what is going on inside. That story is for others to tell.

I'm not talking about the single elected constitution in the EU at certain times representing a kind of half-Parliament, at other occasions a thing that needs to be heard and in the next moment an insignificant nothing. I don't want to explain the different legislation processes, which were applied before the commencement of the Lisbon Treaty: CNS, SYN, AVC, COD. Nor "comitology" with "scrutiny", nor the democratic-historical peculiarity of "initiative reports", with which the Parliament, itself unable to propose legislation, tries to seduce the European Commission to propose legislation instead. Nor the new situation after Lisbon, the novelty of the "ordinary legislative procedure", the revaluation of the Parliament as an equal legislator next to the European Council. Nor the fine print, whereupon the Parliament gets to decide on the organisation of the agricultural market, but not on the prices, subsidies, or agricultural rates. Or whereupon it meets to discuss "measures to strengthen the customs cooperation" but not the amount of the shared customs rates. Please not me, please someone else!

I'm also not talking about the delegates of this parliamentary congregation. I was told many pitiful stories about them. A female scientist wrote her doctorate about the social lives of the delegates and told me that one of them had once broken down in tears during their in-depth interview. One of these constantly travelling delegates had put on record that sometimes, when waking up, he didn't know exactly where he was. In addition, the perpetual mortification for the delegates of being stationed in Brussels and Strasbourg three weeks a month, while at the same time barely anyone back home in the Member States showed any appreciation for their incomprehensible profession. The scientist summed up her six hundred-page doctoral thesis to me: "They're basically just poor sods."

All I'm talking about is the house, the Brusselian "Espace Léopold". Since the EU bores us, most of us are unaware of the fact that this is one of the largest building complexes in the world. The seven central wings alone, which are connected both in-and-externally by twenty-two bridges; cover floor space of 490,000 square metres. Ceauşescu's "People's House" in Bucharest, on occasion considered the largest building in Europe, seems like a doghouse in comparison. All in all the European Parliament covers one million square metres in Brussels, Strasbourg and Luxembourg. The Bucharest palace, also home to a parliament, covers only 364,000.

The European Parliament conceals its actual size. The central block "Altiero Spinelli", with its five seventeen-storey towers and five-level underground parking, is quite the thriller in itself and actually holds several buildings. A ravine of light cuts right through and at the bottom there is a kind of shopping mall with a post office, a hair dresser, a travel agency, branches of several banks, a book store, vending machines for drinks, cakes, ice cream. The way to the cafeteria runs past the gym. There is no swimming pool; luxury is scrupulously avoided.

The twelve single buildings are abbreviated to three letters; individual sections are additionally named with nineteen letters ranging from A to U. The first time I had to go there I was searching amongst the 5,147 Brusselian Parliament rooms for one with the poetical name "PHS00BO1". That could bring anyone to tears. When I arrived, the briefing was almost over.

I mustn't complain, because at my second visit I was escorted by the very house spirit himself. I won't give his name; he is far too well known anyway. The white-haired bow-tie wearer, a former delegate of the Greens, was the alchemist amongst the Brussels lobbyists. He was delivering jokes in four different languages left and right. He said that he had shaken the hands of hundreds of thousands of people in his life. The thought made me woozy.

I couldn't have found a shrewder guide. Rich carpet merchants from Kashmir had only just pooled funds, in return he had organised an exhibition in the Parliament and an image campaign. He showed me a delegate's locker, "whose grandfather had written a book about how to securely place funds on an island". On the locker it read "Stevenson" and the book was called "Treasure Island". My astonishment was much appreciated, and the house spirit fired off his next anecdote.

He explained to me why he liked the European Parliament so much; "because of its flat hierarchies". Even the biggest hot shot, he said, is a "nobody" in this house. At the next occasion I inwardly admitted he was right. I saw the Hungarian politician Viktor Orbán standing in the mall in "ASP", a man who is both hated and loved by millions in several central European countries. He spoke with his companions, a silly red backpack slung over his shoulder. Hundreds of people passed him. No one saw him.

Another time, the house spirit had invited me to a reading, I was yet again hopelessly lost. That night I learned how to triumph over the perhaps largest building in Europe without shedding a single tear. Namely because of the incessant receptions. Signs led "towards a digitalized Europe in 2025", I didn't want to go in that direction. I eventually drank red wine offered by some moustachioed people, which turned out to be Turkish. With some alcohol I could handle being lost a lot better.

It took a while before I surrendered to this city within a city for the first time. Walking on the sound-dampening carpets, I had to repeat to myself what could constitute the fascination for this building: it hosts, after India and followed by the US, the second largest democratically elected parliament in the world. "Second largest parliament in the world", I repeated to myself softly and slightly drunk, "second largest parliament in the world." With time this started to work a little.

The Council

There is a house in Brussels. It is a big house with an endless number of windowless rooms. Four times a year, or even more frequently, the summit of the European heads of state is held here – the European Council. In December 2008, I was there.

In the beginning of my wanderings through the capital I definitely tried to integrate with the European bustle. I obtained a suitable disguise; dark-blue suit, light-blue shirt, dark-blue tie, and put my cuff links on. I visited the three large institutions of the EU: the European Parliament, the European Council and the European Commission. I sat in press conferences and let myself get saturated with "best practice", "biodiversity" and "awareness raising".

At times, boredom fell upon me like manna from heaven, for instance on a Monday, in the Madou Plaza Tower lobby of the European Commission. The Commissioner, who had been recommended to me as the most boring, was opening an exposition on "the Galician language in the context of its linguistic diversity". The designers had been quite creative. There was one installation entitled "semantado palabras" – "sowing words". It was built out of boxes filled with soil. Next to it a wheelbarrow packed with books.

Cleverly enough, the event took place at lunch hour, so at the opening of the buffet the barely twenty visitors had tripled. The Commissioner for Multilingualism at the time, a gaunt Romanian spectacle-wearer, was listening with his hands clasped in front of him, his neck craned, smiling gently. He said that he was "committed" to all languages. He also pronounced himself being in favour of "multi-diversity".

With greater interest I attended the first "Roma Summit" of the EU, a big conference held in the glass palace "Charlemagne". The lunch buffet was outstanding, however the phraseology of the participating civil servants, ministers and NGO officials was soon moving towards a grinding drudgery. I conducted an experiment. I switched my headphones to the language of the people that were the topic of the day.

I didn't know a single word of Romani and only wrote down the terms that I understood from the Roma interpreter's stream of speech: "segregazia, spezialno Romani skola, kindergarten, problema, barriera, negative sentimenta, positivne exempli, europese strukture, Lissabon strategia, sozialno ministero supporto, de-segregazia, aspekto anti-segregazia, kondizialno cash transfer programme, plano anti-segregazia, programmo, solutia, progresso, examinazia, monitoring, effektivno evaluazia, sozialno kohäsia, internationalno projekto, engagemento integratii Romenge, inklusia sozialno, integratia." I was surprised, I understood Romani.

In December, I visited the "Justus Lipsius", the big building hosting the European Council summits. The entrance hall, a towering banner bearing the French presidency floating in the ceiling, was filled with long tables. At the tables, five hundred journalists were sitting in front of five hundred laptops. The same sight all around, in dozens of different rooms. They were all frantically at work. I was the only one wandering idly about.

In the main, such a Council is over quickly. The programme was as follows: on Thursday, meeting between three and seven, group photo, working dinner between eight and ten. On Friday, meeting between ten and one, done. Many journalists had, however, booked their return flights for Saturday. Twenty-seven heads of state, confessional proceedings, haggling until the morning – no one said it out loud. They were all just looking at me knowingly.

The French presidency invited all of us. The cafeteria was open at mealtimes; while upstairs coffee and croissants, sandwiches and water were served. I could sense the taste of honey and walnuts in my Brie sandwich, though I cannot say there was gluttony. For alcohol, the French took money. However, I would not have seen anyone boozing it up, and amongst the thousands of actively working people I only once saw some dally.

I went to the café "Autriche", the only space in the giant building that wasn't repulsive. The barman gave me a fruit salad. In the "Autriche" the glass cage for smokers almost had human dimensions.

A sly old fox addressed me. I acted out my meagre knowledge and asked: "Isn't the *Financial Times* closest? They've got twenty people in Brussels." – "That might be true", the Frenchman replied, "the British and Irish boys from the Commissioners for Trade and Competition pass it all to the Financial Times. But other rules apply at the Council. You have to stick to your own country. You have to make sure to get a First Draft."

I was eavesdropping in the centre aisle of the entrance hall. "We accompanied this statement", someone said in German. It was the head of the Committee on Constitutional Affairs in the European Parliament. Poor him, I thought, where others might accompany women, this guy accompanies statements.

Later on, a chubby advisor of the Polish president stood in the centre aisle. He was sweating and talking nervously, however not about the meeting. Two-dozen Polish journalists were closing in on the plump man with a brutal enthusiasm. Paradoxically, they all made really bored faces.

Towards eleven o'clock at night I found myself suddenly under stress. After the meeting had ended, up to twenty-seven heads of state made statements to the press at the same time. Where should someone like me go? I went down to a narrow basement room, to the Slovakian Prime minister. He had once called journalists "mental bums", so I could therefore hope for him to be brief. Afterwards, I made it to the wine buffet in the hotel "Sofitel", and to a cheerful Austrian chancellor. Indeed, it began and ended later, I was proud of my slyness.

On Friday, I went back to the big house. The Polish advisor was still sweating and the journalists were still sitting largely grouped by country. That could take a while. I went to have a bite in the cafeteria. Three security guards, speaking in French, sat down next to me. "Sarkozy needs to leave at three", one of them said, "he has an event later in France." I spooned my soup quicker.

Shortly after, everything sped up. I hurried to where the former President of the European Council would hold his final vitaminised emo show. Sarkozy indicated why this ending would be on schedule. He said that you couldn't allow for someone saying the same things twice. And anyway, Europe needs "less formalism, badges, accreditation", less of this "deadly boredom in certain meetings".

It was over. The screens in "Autriche" displayed the short red carpet that now no head of state walked on anymore. The journalists lingered. Watching people work was stupid to me, I left the big house. I didn't see any reason to return.

Coffee House Feature

I couldn't really explain why I found myself sitting more and more often in the least alluring café in Brussels, on the ground floor of the headquarters of the European Commission. Not that there weren't any pubs out in the city. Alessia showed me the best bars; the depraved charm of the taverns mollified me, besides, the Belgian monarchy allegedly held the record of most Michelin stars per capita.

However, I lingered more and more often in this most European of all European institutions, in the European Commission. In its headquarters "Berlaymont" I could easily orient myself, unlike in the Parliament the access policies were the same every day, and in general did this harmonising apparatus, untroubled by elections, exert some kind of perverse power of fascination on me.

Three rituals of the apparatus quickly caught my eye: the lunch meeting, the six-thirty-reception and the unveiling of logos. Whoever wants to get ahead, preferably uses every lunch hour to spin a network web. During the six-thirty-reception, which follows working hours and is attended without partners, two-dozen contacts can be made and three to seven business cards exchanged. The Commission acts through programmes, each programme receives a logo, making the ceremonial unveiling of the logo the visual culmination of the *workflow* for the civil servants. My guess is, out in the Member States not everybody would find that hot.

And still I sat more and more often in this cafeteria, from which it was impossible to carve a coffee house feature to save one's life. No service at the table, the visit began with standing in line at the bar, the sad outdoor smoking shed could only be accessed with a badge through a secured door. The employees of the outsourced operating company cashed uneven sums: 1.03 euros for a cappuccino. A little poster sensitised the guests to topics like the "EU Sustainable Energy Week".

The cafeteria's clientele was pure. EU officialdom met here, very formally dressed, to conduct a restrained rational discourse. In my capacity as European Carrie Bradshaw, I didn't have much to report on pan-European flirtatiousness until then. I was thus pretty excited when I once observed an encounter that looked like jiggery-pokery to me. It even smelled a little of sex.

In general, the cafeteria chat was of a kind one would gladly ignore. "Basically, what the Commission does", I heard in front of me. From behind, "communicating with the citizens". The one time I curiously eavesdropped, I was sitting at the separating glass front. I was looking into the crook of the Berlaymont building's arm, into an empty paved courtyard, with bare saplings and light wells. In the background the LEX glass palace came to an end, grey sky. The grey, glassy, silvery prospect was only broken up by the outline of the demolished "Résidence palace"; lacerated, threadbare, brown. Perhaps I was sitting more and more frequently in this café because its totality appealed to me. You could look as hard as you wanted, you would see nothing but EU.

It was around three o'clock, the cafeteria was half empty. Our hero was a regular, a small, rotund spectacle-wearing man in a suit, over fifty. He looked a bit like Elton John, but without the colourfulness of his accessories. The heroine was under thirty and quite pretty. She had braided her blond hair, was wearing numerous silvery bangles, her fingernails were painted red. I had never seen a woman with red nail polish in the Commission cafeteria before. Her fingernails alone, in the midst of the orderly office folk, had the look of sin itself.

They were both British, him and her. The young woman spoke with a moderate cockney accent. Her frivolous shopping-mall style didn't fit in with this place. Did she want to fit in somehow?

I learned from the scraps of conversation drifting by that the gentleman was entertaining the girlie with a thick array of gruesome stories. He began with the Scottish middle ages, changed to Idi Amin and escalated to the joke: "I should kill you." He served the punch lines dryly; at the moment of delivery he keenly raised his eyebrows.

The young woman had a sensuous and guttural laugh. While he sat in front of her like an acolyte, she turned back and forth on her revolving chair, letting him see her black stocking-wearing legs. "What about my shoes?" she asked and raised her boots. I was all agog. What could she want from this civil servant?

She was drinking diet coke through a straw; the can must have been long empty by now. By degrees I discovered the trick. She sucked the coke through the white straw, barely wet her lips and let the liquid flow back into the can.

The gentleman finally got down to the girlie's concerns. "A good CV will get your foot in the door", he said, "it's all presentation." He also advised her to choose italics, font size 14 for the introduction, font size 12 for the rest. It wasn't any more corrupt than that. And yet, by the standards of the Commission cafeteria it was incredibly hot.

The Fat

After the smokers came the fat, that was my impression. The British press proposed to present fattening foods with deterring photos, along the lines of cigarette packages shocking with pictures of damaged lungs. A "White Paper" from the European Commission demanded that the trend towards obesity be reversed by 2015 at the latest.

In Brussels I heard scattered announcements, for instance about the creation of a new profession. Since consumers "need professional advice in order to do their shopping with awareness", thirteen universities now trained "European Masters in Consumer Affairs". During one Commission briefing an English journalist asked with adept aspiration for "life-style assessment". I took notice. I promised myself not to rest before I could face the central brain of the anti-fat movement.

I have to start by saying that I am thin myself; however, I like fat people. Staszek for example I wouldn't have called fat, but the particular stoutness of his appearance filled me with trust. Kick-starting lunch meetings quickly became too strenuous for me; I mostly ate in the European Commission cafeteria. There the nutrient table was written in larger print than the prices. Yet I was missing something else. For a long time I couldn't figure out what it was. Then it hit me: a room full of civil servants, not one of them was fat.

I couldn't believe it, so I conducted censuses in the main cafeterias of the European institutions. In the Commission only four out of a hundred people could be called stout, in the Council four out of a hundred, in the Parliament three out of a hundred. Does a battle start here, I asked myself, lean against fat?

I attended a podium discussion in the European Parliament organised by the International Butchers' Confederation. The Health Commissioner read out her proposition, which stated that in future an elaborate list of information must be printed on all packaging. "Nutrition profiling", on the front, at least three millimetres in size. After the statement the strict Cypriot Commissioner vanished and was replaced by her staff. All of her staff had Greek, or perhaps Greek-Cypriot names.

The officials of the Butchers' Confederation were alarmed. One was suspicious of the proposed regulation of Designation of Origin and posed a trick question: were the Germans still allowed to call a sausage, which verifiably didn't come from Vienna, a "Vienna sausage"? The Greeks on the podium walked right into the trap: you could perhaps rename this sausage "a Viennese style sausage".

The buffet following the discussion was the meatiest I had experienced in my year in Brussels. Staszek joined me at the buffet. I summed up what I had learned so far about the actions taken by the EU against obesity. He reacted in his own way, with a light, sad, introverted shake of the head.

I probably asked him the question that I would aim at him even more emphatically later on: "Don't you Poles want to save Europe yet again?" We liked to chat like that. From Staszek's point of view, the Poles had saved Europe at least three times in history; I tried to beat him down to two. Freeing Vienna from the Turks in 1683 and disrupting the Communist Empire until 1989, I found that heroic enough. But where were the Poles now? It was perhaps a bit of a tall order to expect the Poles to fix it again. I could tell by Staszek's facial expression that he didn't want to save Europe. He wanted a woman.

I got a tip that the sought-after central brain of the anti-fat movement was to be found in Luxembourg. I had to go there, for better or for worse. That meant three hours by train from Brussels and still I hadn't arrived at my destination; the "DG Health, Unit C-4" was situated on an arterial road. An industrial park, a sanitary supplies' store, next to it an aluminium-coloured office building. I was there.

Two middle-aged civil servants sat opposite me at a small conference table, one Lorrainer with a slightly reddened face and one very lean bespectacled Pole who mostly remained silent. The Lorrainer explained initially that an Anti-Obesity-Team in the EU didn't exist. Obesity is a disease, and the responsibility for diseases lies with the Member States. That's why the department is called "Health Determinants", he explained further. Two-dozen civil servants worked on the requirements for a healthy life-style, two or three on obesity. Two of them were sitting opposite me. I was right.

The Lorrainer, who previously had been working in drug fighting, warned me about Cyprus: "Cyprus is the centre of Mediterranean cuisine, yet it has one of the highest rates of obese children." If this trend wasn't stopped, the health systems would collapse. "That doesn't just entail individual pain, but costs as well."

He spoke calmly and firmly, the measures taken up until this point weren't radical enough for him. I asked him: "Is it about informing or educating people?" – "Both", he replied. He felt it absolutely appropriate to educate adults. He didn't want to appear fanatic: "I'm no priest, I'm a good soldier."

After the talk I headed to the Luxembourg City centre. I went to the tavern "beim Änder", it was already full at five o'clock. "Luxembourgish" was spoken all around me, "adi!" people called out when they left, and I didn't see a single pillar of the health system amongst the guests.

I had a "Mettwurst", that sounded fat, and flushed it down with plenty red wine while imbibing the dense second-hand smoke with relish. A tape with German Schlager music was playing. When the German song "Junge, komm bald wieder" – "Boy, come back soon!" – came on, the Luxembourgers started singing along. "I worry", the people to my right sang. "I worry about you", the people to my left sang back.

At the Meat Market

The Estonian-Romanian novel starts off with me managing to set up a coffee date in Brussels with an Estonian woman. There aren't many Estonians, barely one million not counting the Estonian Russians, which meant I really had to make this one count.

Making it count with small nations was my motto at first anyway. I had promised the newspapers that I would portray all European nations. Behind it lay the assumption that the European bubble would potentially consist of national sub-bubbles. Therefore I fervently tried to find pubs, clubs and associations, particularly for smaller nations.

I noticed however that the representatives of the really small peoples constantly claimed that a thousand members of their respective people were living in Brussels. The only exception was the representative of the internationally not-recognised "Turkish Republic of Northern Cyprus", who received me with Mediterranean vitality, and invited me to sit in a leather armchair facing the prestigious shopping street "Louise". He claimed that there were only ten Turkish Cypriots living in Brussels.

I attempted to study several nations. I spent a couple of days in one member country, which at that time had only just been saved from total bankruptcy, Latvia. There was a petition set up online that had caused quite the commotion, in which it was suggested that Latvia should apply for occupation by Sweden, since the Latvian banks were under Swedish control anyhow. An astonishing number of jokesters had actually signed it. I wanted to extend my experiences from the cold, quiet and ruined Riga, and relive them in the European capital. That resulted in nothing at all. The Latvians didn't even have their own pub in Brussels. The Swedes were notorious for their preference for the pub "Fat Boys". The "Fat Boys" were popular thanks to a cheap trick; they were broadcasting football matches from the big European leagues. I didn't find any Swedes though. However, they couldn't possibly have been as impressive as the Swedish businessman I came across in ice-cold Riga, who was shouting loudly: "I also signed a petition – for Sweden not to give any more money to Latvia!"

I followed up on the phenomenon that everyone in Europe prefers counting themselves to the West, but that central Europe in its capacity as a time zone devours a wide part of the West. For instance, on the northwest Spanish peninsula at Cape Finisterre the sun doesn't reach its highest peak until at 2:37 pm, which means that the children go to school in the dark. This made me think of the Galicians, whose nationalist party demanded the implementation of Greenwich Mean Time. The leading Galician Nationalist in Brussels described her country to me with flailing hand gestures. "Galicia is closed off from the rest of Spain", she said. "The light is different, it rains a lot, it's often foggy, it's actually quite like Ireland." She admitted that the Spanish parliament had shot down the idea of the change of time zone. She still fought on though, now in Brussels with an always-appreciated argument: optimising time zones saves energy.

I visited the smallest region with its own legislation in the EU, a "sub-national constituency" taking up 0.75 percent of Belgium; the "German-speaking Community of Belgium". That too was nice and interesting on a federalist level. I had admittedly imagined an even nicer place, earlier, at home in my Slovakian suburb when I was studying the online version of the German-Belgian newspaper *Grenz-Echo*. Back then, I was wondering about certain German-Belgian words, about "side people" in "provincial palaces", about "church factories" and about "language baths" that proceeded nicely. I love bathing in languages. I don't have to understand them, not the languages, and not the language baths either.

Most of the people were nice to me, however the Greenlanders really weren't. They left the European Communities in 1985, and during my time in Brussels I heard rumours that they would perhaps be leaving Denmark as well. I turned to Greenland's representation in search for an answer, and for a long time didn't get anywhere. The official email address was discontinued, when I called them the switchboard told me that the Greenlanders "should be coming in anytime now" or "must have just left". At one point I heard a voice in the line, a member of the Danish minority in Greenland. This woman, Ms Sørensen, said that they were undergoing an upheaval and that I had to wait for the arrival of the new manager. That sounded like heads were rolling. I wanted to pop over there for a look, but Ms Sørensen strictly forbade me to come. So I went even more determined than ever.

It was an office building next to the Danish representation, right in the centre of Gotham City. A flag with a polar bear indicated that I had come to the right place. I had arrived right at peak working hour. I didn't ring the doorbell but slipped in behind a serious-looking gentleman. All the occupants of the building were listed inside the lift; "Greenland Representation" was situated on the first floor. I pressed "1" but nothing happened. All the other floors were accessible, just not Greenland. I got out on "3", an extremely tidy and empty floor housing the accordingly over-autonomous Faroe Islands. "Is this Greenland?" I asked sanctimoniously. "No, everyone over there should have gone home by now."

Back in the lift I noticed a small metal plate, designated to Greenland. I pressed in that general area, nothing happened. Then I noticed a spark of light from a dark camera lens inside the metal plate. Heavens almighty, went through my head, were the Greenlanders filming me? Had the polar people been observing me this whole time? I started to feel a bit uneasy. I tried going down the emergency staircase, but in vain, even the emergency exit was blocked to the Greenlander floor. I concluded that the Greenlanders didn't want to be portrayed.

I started to doubt myself. My concept of presenting the peoples of Europe through the prism of Brussels' European bubble resulted only in conspicuously fruitless material. Would Carrie Bradshaw have discarded my approach, and considered it too dimwitted? What's more, small nations usually presented themselves with folk music and dancing. There was a Slovenian wine tasting event for example, with Slovenian wine queens, and as the wine queens filled up our glasses they would say in English: "This is my wine."

I felt reluctant to write about folklore. I then would have to write about Styrian soft rock in the Styrian representation and about a Saturday night in Liège where I had gone out of curiosity to socialise with dancing Slovakian Eurocrat women. The scene took place in the culture centre of a degrading suburb. The closely spaced red brick houses reminded me of worker ghettos in central England, and of the burned-out jets of flames between the smoking chimneys in Dniprodzerzhynsk. The evening was long, the company of thirty had been rehearsing for at least thirty years, there were both Hungarian and Slovakian folk dances being performed. Afterwards, I was told that the dances were performed almost exclusively by Belgians. They didn't understand a single word of what they sung in the lookout-for-a-wife songs.

I had the increasing feeling that the intimate national circles in the Valley of the Eurocrats weren't noteably distinctive, and realised that I had to do with a unique species; a unique Homo Brusselian. I abandoned the idea of portraying particular nations from a Brusselian perspective. That was only possible with people who were established in Brussels, and had a rich history of migration, for example the Italians, the Portuguese, the Moroccans and the Albanians. I had to change my approach.

And thus, I'm back to square one. I'm back to having coffees with the Estonian woman, back to having full-bodied talks of an Estonian-Romanian novel. The Estonian's name was Tiina. She was in her early forties, blond and tall. Her English, along with her clothing, had a casual and somewhat mannered elegance. Naturally, she said that there were a thousand Estonians in Brussels. I would find a couple of them in the Irish pub "Wild Geese". Naturally, I never approached any of these uninteresting wild geese. I wanted to talk to Tiina about the Estonians, about these internet-infatuated prodigies, who were still taking out loans via text messages as the crisis broke out.

In the next instant, I was staring at the EU official in disbelief. "I feel like a parasite", she said. She claimed that Eurocrats were parasites and only attracted other Belgian parasites. All I needed to do was to go to "place Lux", to place du Luxembourg, on a Friday night to get a taste of that. "One great meat market", Tiina called it, "even girls from Antwerp go there to find themselves a Eurocrat."

That was like a challenge. I immediately went there. Place Lux is a former station forecourt in front of the abundant complex of the European Parliament, which started out as a building complex on the current underground Luxembourg station. The square was small, situated in the old part of town, with neatly arranged two-storey bourgeois houses. I went there on the last warm autumn night of the year. There were a couple of bars with hundreds of young people standing in front, the crowd virtually spilling into the city buses stopping at the square.

I had a Eurocrat with me, outstanding bait. A salary towards six thousand, a life-long contract, a gold credit card and single. His name was Staszek. It wasn't his first time at the "place", as you say it in French, and his expectations were slightly lower than mine. He knew some people. One, an internationally oriented Belgian guy who pronounced his first name in an Anglo-Saxon way. "Staszek" turned into "stay sick"!

Place Lux was indeed an all-European get-together of young and attractive people. Spontaneously, I didn't like them all that much, however, with Tiina's announcement in mind, it still turned out to be eminently decent. Staszek, being anything but shy, spoke to a lot of people. We asked them where they came from. One guy from Antwerp was there, apparently the girls from Antwerp had been held up. Stay Sick didn't manage to catch a single fish.

I followed another piece of advice. "Mirano" was a nightclub that had been made fashionable with draped white cloth, and every Thursday invited guests to a dance of the Eurocrats. I went there with Liliana, the bored intellectual Romanian. The guests were stylish. The women were inconspicuous; the men were styled over the top.

I was eyeing one guy, so nice were his trousers and so nice was his shirt. It turned out that he was Romanian, and that Liliana knew him. She quickly badmouthed him, and then introduced us. Alexandru, in his late twenties, seemed all right with the distraction, because a delicate Latina, who he had apparently rejected in the past, kept trying to gently snuggle up against him.

I asked Alexandru where he had bought his nice clothes. "In London, Covent Garden", he replied and added kindly: "If you go there for closing sales you can find a shirt for twenty-five pounds." I gazed down at my own dark-blue suit, in fact bought at C&A's sales, and then looked at Alexandru; driving a BMW, living on the prestigious boulevard Louise. I thought: even though Romanians pay twice as much for loan instalments as the inhabitants of the euro zone, they look good doing it!

We danced. One girl appealed to Alexandru, a bouncing girl with emerald-green feline eyes wearing a respectable skirt and a respectable blouse. She looked like she was having the time of her life. He was hoping that she was Russian and danced slowly but surely towards her. "She's Estonian", he announced as he was dancing back towards me, "she speaks Russian though." Baffled, he added: "She thinks she's ugly." Next thing, the Estonian was being twirled about by an Indian guy. Alexandru watched them, suffering. Liliana, who previously had described Alexandru as racist, enjoyed watching him suffer.

Alexandru had gotten her number though. We took our leave, and there was no one to tell me how the little novel of the relationship between Estonia and Romania would end, between the Committee of the Regions and the legal department of the Commission; until I crossed paths with Alexandru in the Commission's cafeteria.

From the outset he declared the story a "closed case". He had helped the Estonian girl putting an IKEA bed together, but then he had danced with someone else in "Mirano" and the Estonian had chased him away. Alexandru was however only a tad sad about it. He said that he had found a genuine Russian girl.

The Centre

She was young and friendly, quite tall for a Spaniard, her gold-blond hair and hazelnut gaze inspired confidence. Her name was Claudia. I wasn't sure whether I was engaged in a flirt or just some kind of incredibly skilful strategy of communication.

Our first encounter only lasted a couple of minutes. Claudia worked for a lobby for hire and spoke to me at one of those events, during which the business style of the European Commission was merged with the NGO style of image-conscious corporations to climaxes of phraseology of sustainability. On that very day, a high-ranked Commission official and representatives from Carrefour and Tetra Pak had only good things to say about each other. I was given an energy-saving bulb.

Claudia's event was part of a series called: "More than 150 key stakeholders invite you to take a week to change tomorrow." Thanks to a concept, which originally derived from business economics, the European Commission had managed to detect more than a hundred and fifty of such "stakeholders". Stakeholder was the win-win concept of the season. Whoever didn't have stakeholders, quickly had to acquire some.

Claudia was attractive; she had a tendency to blush. Her company lobbied for abominable businesses like *Google*, and at the same time she called herself a "defender of human rights". Then I saw her business card. The lobby for hire was called "The Centre", symbolised by mystical intertwined rings. I was drawn to it in a hypnotic way. Who, if not this gentle and caring centre, would give me the orientation I had longed for? I just had to go there.

My query may have been a little too enthusiastic, but in any case Claudia agreed with the side note that she had been happily together with her boyfriend for seven years. I arrived at "The Centre" on a late afternoon. It was an old Brusselian bourgeois building in a prime location; the big blue "Centre" banner with the intertwined white rings was flying in the wind.

A charming black little elf took me up a narrow staircase. On the first floor, she showed me to a lounge chair and then disappeared. Claudia was letting me wait. I was alone. I felt uncomfortably out of place. As if I had ended up with a cult that didn't want me.

I left my seat. In the lobby on the first floor everything that was important had been posted on the wall: "Forum" led to human rights, "Consultancy" to money, "Air" to windows, "Water" to the toilets. Appetisers were being served for the evening gathering. I sneaked up to a roll of prosciutto ham. Suddenly, the green-covered wooden floor unexpectedly creaked loudly at the other end of the room. I went back to the meeting room.

Then Claudia came. She was smiling as she had the first time we'd met. We sat down in the lounge chairs and started chatting. Claudia finally proved to be a prototype of the Homo Brusselian: studied at the College of Europe in Bruges, European law, got a boyfriend. Worked for the European Parliament's Press Service, collected media contacts, and since then in "The Centre". Sheltering Catalan parents, her father "a great architect".

On this workday, Claudia had brought representatives for an agricultural organisation together with some journalists. Unpaid dedication to African child soldiers and then canvassing for Tetra Pak, she did by no means see that as a contrast. "Our input is very valuable to the institutions."

As the conversation got somewhat more convivial, Claudia suddenly leapt up. No, this wasn't a flirt; she had to "finish writing a health check on agricultural policy". She dropped me off at the exclusive house gathering.

People were sitting at a conference table, each one behind their little nametag, and some first class British Liberal Democrats were stipulating the introduction of the euro in the United Kingdom. "I salute your efforts", a Mr Watson cried out to a Mr Stevens. I enjoyed the English of the two gentlemen; normally I was exposed to the English of non-British Eurocrats that in an effort of elegance mostly became long-winded.

Mr Anderson, the British manager of "The Centre" was moderating. The following morning, in the European

Parliament, the circles were closed. Mr Anderson again moderating, this time a presentation of the European Ombudsman. And the European Ombudsman, an agile Greek professor, could also already refer to stakeholders.

The Albanians

Trouble was definitely to be expected. On the one hand, trouble with discrimination opponents, since my visit with the Brussels Albanians ended at an Albanian dealer's. Trouble on the other hand with the Albanian dealer, since he didn't want to go to prison for the third time because of me.

And yet I am fascinated. The Albanians are, next to the Roma, the last Europeans who still foster a large number of children. I listen with delight to their language, which they call "the first European language". No Albanian state is a member of the EU, but they've been in the capital for a long time. There are thirty thousand Albanians living in Brussels, half of which probably come from Kosovo and Macedonia.

First, I went to an Albanian cultural festival. The Belgian artist Alessia accompanied me. Walking through Saint Gilles with Alessia always filled me with the pleasant illusion of being completely integrated in the Belgian kingdom. Alessia would be greeted from left to right, it seemed like she knew everyone. I was sorry to lose sight of her for a while after this night. She didn't have it easy, she had a very different map of Brussels in her head. Because of her hot-blooded lovers, many streets were off limits with a manly companion.

As we were walking on a safe route towards the Albanian cultural festival, Alessia started to brag. She said that she could show me a café where I could find an Albanian killer. "Fifty euros for a shot to the head, fifteen euros for a shot in the knee." I didn't believe a word she said. But that is how people talk about Albanians.

The cultural festival painted a different picture of them. Hundreds of people were streaming into a sombre culture centre, amongst them were a couple of dignitaries with shortly bound ties, a couple of young men in black leather jackets, predominantly respectable citizens. They were fawning about the Albanian minister of culture, an authority figure wearing a crimson striped tie. In the packed auditorium, people were listening to the historical account of a white-haired professor. Standing behind him were three girls in traditional costumes. They were standing all throughout the lively public discussion.

Somewhere I had picked up that the Albanians are divided into two tribes, Ghegs and Tosks, and that we therefore didn't have to fear the idea of a greater Albania too much. I spoke about this with the dynamic organiser of the cultural festival. "We're indeed currently living in three states", he retorted, but my question was based on "false information". The Albanians are a united people.

Secondly, I went to an Albanian café in the Albanian neighbourhood in the Schaerbeek quarter. The floor was tiled white; the sitting benches were clad in light blood-red cloth. There were no women and no ladies' toilets; the beer was, to Staszek's pleased astonishment, only one euro. At times, Staszek's astonishment astonished me on such excursions. He said that he would never have discovered this pure Albanian world if it wasn't for my initiative. That in turn astonished me, barely any other Eurocrat roamed Brussels and the Belgian provinces as thoroughly as my unhappy Polish mate. This evening he at least seemed to enjoy his Belgian exile. We talked to the guys at the bar. Behold, there they were. Ghegs and Tosks peacefully united. I asked how many brothers they had. They had between two and six.

Thirdly, I called on the Albanian dealer. I only dare to reveal this much about him: he was in his early thirties, good-looking, and had a striking aura. I promised not to name his neighbourhood. It was one of the better ones. I asked him to choose a name for himself. He made us some green tea.

In truth I had called on Skander in order to explore the peculiarities of the people he labelled the "European community" through the prism of drug use. He had three hundred costumers who bought Dutch cannabis from him, many of whom were Eurocrats. The Eurocrats, Skander said, were different from other costumers in but one aspect: "They have more money. That's why they mostly buy twice as much, thirty grams for two hundred euros."

He was an efficient individual. Back in the days he brought glamour to the neighbourhood, when he was doing and dealing coke and living with a Tahitian high-class prostitute. That's all in the past, he emphasised. In any case, he maintained that he had never been a pimp. He only sold the weed that he smoked himself, he pointed out. Thus he made less money than before, however he preferred leading a safer life.

At one point he leaned slightly forward and softly said: "You know, I'm a charmer, a seducer." Many of his clients were women. But he didn't have sex with them. He had long since removed himself from the "Albanian community", he said, "for security reasons". His mother called him a Belgian but he felt like an Albanian: "Albanians have never mingled much with other peoples. I can even sense an Albanian walking behind me."

He didn't know whether he was Gheg or Tosk, but I already had the image of the Albanians to be an agreeable people. And I get along with them. Honestly, people, I'm not looking for trouble.

The Portuguese

Oh, this wandering, roving, migrating! In the sixties, Portuguese people were streaming towards the north, fleeing from poverty, military service and dictatorship. They still left in the eighties. Shortly after, Portugal itself took on immigrants, from Africa, Latin America and Eastern Europe. Within a decade the population of the Iberian Peninsula increased – only through immigration – by five and a half million people.

In the city of Brussels, 25,000 Portuguese people have stayed on. I made my way to "Orfeu", their cultural centre, just behind the tall buildings of the European institutions. The bookshop had a strong aroma of a parish library and at the till there were two old and grey Portuguese women doing inventory. "The ladies are working for free", the director told me, "this is not a business."

The director, Joaquim Pinto da Silva, was a sophisticated gentleman dressed in corduroy. He had come to Brussels in 1984, working as a Commission official, and then in 1989 he had founded the Brusselian memorial for writer Fernando Pessoa. He was still working at the Commission; "Orfeu" was just his hobby. It was hard to win over the established Portuguese working class for his cultural programme, he said; "my best costumers are EU-officials".

I went to the well-known Portuguese neighbourhood, above the "Flagey", around rue de la Brasserie. Winding and mounting side streets and closely spaced brick houses with black wrought-iron balconies. The houses were built by Belgians and the many Portuguese pubs fitted nicely into the scenery. Da Silva had introduced me to Portuguese aesthetics: the Pessoa memorial was surrounded by small black and white cobblestones. The tiling, which normally covered facades in Portugal, could be found amongst the Brusselian Portuguese as well, namely inside the highly praised bakery "Garcia". Old men were sitting in the Portuguese cafés, wearing pullovers over their shirts, reading. That is what you could call a successfully integrated diversity.

I had never been to that country whose sibilant sounding nasal language is said to resound the speaker's longing of the sea. I took a cheap flight to Faro. On board, I read Pessoa: "Travel is for those who cannot feel." That hit home.

I arrived in the Algarve on a January evening. It was raining but Nordic people immediately felt that special southern spirit. With Pessoa's "Book of Disquiet" under my arm, I took a stroll all alone under glistening wet palm trees. The day after, the sun shone on the evergreen urban vegetation, I grabbed some oranges from the orange trees in front of the tower-less cathedral. In the port, behind the white boats and green palm trees, rusty regional trains were passing by.

All around me were retired Northerners. One million Brits had settled in Spain alone, *El País* reported. The people I saw were denim retirees, they were still very active. I sat down in the coffee shop "Alianca", the subtle white stucco on the roof reminded me of the Brusselian "Orfeu". I was sitting amongst idle Portuguese people, amongst customers who had accomplished the coffee shop art by spending hours reading, smoking and observing, just like I would do at home. A Flemish denim retiree ran through the door: "Where's the exhibition, where are the photos from the world war?" She ran on for a while longer.

Oh, these eternal migrations! Everywhere I went migrants surrounded me. On Saturday night, after a rain shower in the evergreen winter, I witnessed a scene on the harbour promenade, which I found strangely sad. A woman, who turned out to be a fifty-year old Moldavian, was looking after a child, a Portuguese three-year old.

The little boy was sitting on a colourful plastic vehicle and was going around in circles on the black and white pavement. He didn't dignify his caretaker with one single look. He resolutely made his way wherever he wanted. It was after eleven o'clock at night. The Moldavian woman, wearing a Soviet-style winter coat, was trotting morosely after the boy.

The Finns

Once I visited a sauna located in a vicarage. The fact that it was possible to sauna-bathe in the basement of a vicarage, and that this exclusive men-only evening was called "Adam", had awoken my particular interest. Curtain's drawn for the Brusselian Finns!

The two or three thousand Finns living in Brussels had established numerous saunas, such as in the hotel "Scandic" or on the top floor of the Finnish representation. The men's sauna in the "Brysselin pappila", the "Seamen's Mission", always on the first Wednesday of the month, consisted of a quite modest group. "Adam" took place between 7 and 8:30 pm, in total five to seven men showed up. They had to be out of there by 9 pm since that was when the refectory cafeteria above was closing, with all its carefully presented range of Finnish foods.

My general interest was dedicated to the pure Finnish sauna doctrine. I had myself been schooled in a sauna in the winter of 2004, in the Kiev struck by the triumphant

Orange Revolution. At that time I found saunas disgusting, and I went reluctantly. I then sat in a small wooden sweat chamber with a group of friends, all young people, in the very proximity to some exceptionally attractive Ukrainian women. "Don't start with politics now!" one of them whispered to me, "Volodja supported Yanukovych."

Volodja was not only a supporter of the succumbing part of the revolution, but also somewhat of a sauna professional. When he noticed the novice, he immediately started instructing me. The fact that he was birching me in front of the stark naked beauties seemed to be a useful experience. However, he then took me out of the boiling heat and got me into a man-deep basin, and wouldn't let me out of the freezing water for three whole minutes. He stood at the pool's edge and preached down at me: "You have to conquer the cold from within." He indeed looked like a conqueror then.

Afterwards, I felt as if born again. Since then I frequently go to the sauna, although clearly more Roman, with softer transitions between hot and cold. And lo and behold – in the club-inspired basement of the Brusselian Finnish vicarage there was no cold basin. On this evening there were two or three EU-officials in the sauna, also one long-haired Erasmus student and a bulky pensioner with a purring joy of life, who was planning to relocate to the South of France. They were all Finns, very hospitable, and they would often refrain from speaking Finnish for my sake.

The organiser, a family man called Jaako Aarnio, had a trusting disposition. He spoke respectfully of the Finnish pastors. The last one had founded the sauna three years ago, and had brought the stones for the oven over the Nordic seas all by himself. The new pastor originally came from drug counselling, which was a big help in view of the Belgian schools.

Regarding the Finnish sauna, Jaako said that: "There are no fixed rules." Some customs nevertheless caught my attention. For instance, the Finnish sauna is not unisex, however there were no discernible homoerotic vibes during the all-male "Adam" evening. In the beginning they all took some foil from a dispenser, put it down with the plastic side to the hot wood and then sat down on the papered side. They kept pouring water onto the stones fervently. The ventilation system is the actual secret, Jaako explained to me. During the breaks they drank beer. They raved about their smoke saunas at home, filled with an infectious enthusiasm. "Afterwards, you jump into the lake", one of them said. As if every Finn had a lake in front of their door.

I felt comfortable in the refectory; the Finns knew how to do well for themselves here in Brussels. They were only cruel when commenting the sauna culture of other countries. I heard the following being said about a Spanish sauna: "The people had their clothes on, the sauna only had forty or fifty degrees, some read. Such saunas should be forbidden by law." Jaako Aarnio convulsed, even twenty-eight years later, when he spoke of a sauna that he once experienced in Vienna in 1981: "There was a sign on the door saying 'Grilling Room'."

As much as I liked them, I still remained dedicated to Volodja in one aspect: I need the cold, to conquer it from within. And there was nothing to be conquered amongst the Finns.

The Civil Servants

There were times when I cursed myself, when I wanted to scream, when I wanted to run. Sometimes I cursed myself for having chosen the Valley of the Eurocrats of all places as the foraging ground of a European Carrie Bradshaw. Wasn't it in Ukrainian nights and amongst Slovakian gypsies that my core had been shaken, my mind had been stimulated, my heart stirred, my soul uplifted? Where was my place in this citadel of harmonisation? Which cruel animal experiment had I exposed myself to in full possession of human free will?

Sure, power was exercised in Brussels. Sure, seventy or eighty percent of the legislation. Sure, it wasn't a coincidence that fifteen to thirty-five thousand lobbyists were influencing the decision-making processes. But damn it, I was up against civil servants.

These civil servants were decent, team-oriented, transparent and communicative. They took long showers, dressed properly, answered emails. They didn't flaunt any kind of distinct masculinity or any exposed femininity.

They were well tempered in every respect. They didn't wear any over-sleeves, they were modern, they were elite civil servants in the full meaning of the expression. Although less than half of the sixty thousand were official, the civil servants shaped the operation, they were hired for life, the civil servants instilled stability.

Surely, I'm being ungrateful. The civil servants received me in a friendly enough manner. A couple of them let me stay at their place, some even for free, and still they made me feel uneasy. I pull out a business card from the pile; business cards fell on my head like drizzle out of the Belgian sky. I reach for a Slovakian civil servant's card. His first name was "Dušan" which derives from "duša", the Slavic word for soul. The civil servant called himself "Dusan" though, he had dropped the little roof over the s, the spelling now reminding me of the Slovakian word stem for choking. Had he accidentally lost his soul? And damn it, what did I expect? That the many different nations were something special here? Where should the rational-international life stories end if not in the Eurocrat valley?

I remember their English. They spoke it really well, much better than I did, even if it was a standardised midstream of the language, without excited highs and solid lows. I remember Facebook and Fusion. Not the Fu-si-on of businesses, but Fjoooshn, the blend of agreeable combined cultures conveyed first by gastronomy and now other areas of life.

I remember a dinner in the Uccle quarter, an avenue with front gardens, an upper class house. The hostess was a graceful Maltese woman. My archive of national peculiarities told me that fifty-four percent of the Maltese keep the record number of reading less than one book a year, that they called their Roman Catholic God "Allah" in Maltese, and that they, the Maltese men, have a tendency to masturbate in front of German female tourists on the beaches of their island. However, I was on the wrong track with this archive. I didn't find out anything more essential from the Maltese hostess. She didn't want to confirm whether public masturbation was a national tradition or not.

The dinner was held for a group of Eurocrat friends, a motley crew of nations, even an evaluator was present. When the Maltese hostess invited us into the dining room she asked: "Shall we migrate?" That was certainly well said, the graceful hostess could almost be considered a native speaker. I thought to myself: with friends I go over there, with friends I don't migrate.

I went to the department which organised the "Concours", the selection of EU personnel. EPSO, an "interinstitutional office", one hundred and fifty employees. I met an official of Flemish origin at EPSO. Salary grade AST8, fifty-one years old, thirty-one years of service for Europe.

He invited me into his small office which went in almost every shade of light grey. He smiled at me broadly, but there was something about him that irritated me. He didn't shake my hand, he just looked distantly over my shoulder. Gradually I understood that the EPSO-official was nearly blind. In front of his keyboard was a long console with creases over which he read lines with his fingertips as nimble as a magician. He spoke the three working languages of the EU fluently; English, French, German. He had a machine to read texts for him. The machine read at a mad pace, completely incomprehensible to me. He understood everything.

I learned that the EU employed 50.88 percent women and 49.12 percent men. The majority was highly educated and most of them were on life-long contracts. They only took on "the best of the best" the EPSO-official said, for a hundred positions there were thousands of applicants. As a result of the economic crisis he anticipated an ever greater rush in 2010. I thought about Liliana, the coy Romanian who was one of those who had just changed focus. At first she had wanted to escape the Helium group and the boredom by looking for a job in Bucharest. That was, despite her outstanding qualifications, quite hopeless. So she decided to stay and started with the admission process to the European Commission which just had been made accessible to Romanians. That would take one whole year.

The EPSO-official explained further: "There are no quotas." No one would ask about religion, politics or sexual orientation. They only enquired about "special needs", as with his visual impairment. Often he added: "That's also written in the official journal." I asked him what makes a good Commission official. "To be able to think logically in a number of languages", he replied, "and to be able to work well in an international environment." One candidate had once admitted that he didn't like one particular Member State, Germany. "When you say that, it's over", the official told me. "You shouldn't say these things, but you can think them."

"We are running policies", the Lorrainer Commission official from the anti-fat movement had said, he was creating something similar to politics. I asked at the EPSO if they screen the applicant's standing point on the politics of the European Union. "We refrain from doing so", said the official.

Before I took my leave, the friendly Fleming stressed the meaning of innovation in the institutions. "The European Year of Creativity and Innovation" had indeed just started. "Are we doing things properly?" he asked rhetorically, "but are we doing the right things properly?" That wasn't really the question that bothered me the most, even though I would have liked to see how a Commission official would have mediated with my eastern Slovakian gypsy friends about the recently communicated ban on big plasma TVs. I asked myself with what legitimacy the Commission is often quite properly handling the often quite right things. I asked myself: who ordered this, who voted for it? Who wanted a Europe where the right of initiative and power of creativity are affiliated with civil servants? Would the peoples of Europe ever want that? Where does it all lead? And what will become of it all?

I didn't ask the helpful EPSO-official any of those things, he wouldn't have been allowed to answer me anyway. I knew that without the understanding of the Commission officials, the real existing shape of Europe wouldn't be comprehensible. But damn it, I had enough. I just wanted to flee. And away I fled, in all kinds of directions. I fled to the transsexuals, I fled to the Africans, I fled into the night.

The Sceptics

Only once was I able to identify clear opponents of the EU in Brussels. It was on a dull autumn day, and a small group of organised demonstrators had assembled in front of the European Commission's headquarters.

They were Irish and French, all young men with short hair. For every demonstrator there was a camera or a microphone. One of them held up an image of a chimpanzee. Above the image it read that a monkey is more prone to change than the EU. They were roaring out catch phrases like "power to the people", loudly, in shambles and in their respective languages. Eventually, they all joined together in a phrase made up by the French, according to the French custom of intonation at the end: "Barrosó Fashó". I found the demonstrators ridiculous. To call the cuddly Portuguese President of the European Commission a fascist sounded like a scene from a Charlie Chaplin movie.

Then however, as I implied earlier, the Eurocrat milieu started to get to me. I acknowledged having hostile feelings towards it. Outwardly, I had adjusted to these people,

I even put on a dark-blue knitted tie acquired in Portugal. With it, I stood on the inconspicuous side.

I saw myself doing remarkable things. I bought a Czech newspaper from the well-assorted newsstand in the ASP mall inside the European Parliament. With the Czech newspaper I sat down in the Parliament bar Mickey Mouse and read with relish about the Czech president's pranks directed towards the Treaty of Lisbon. Václav Klaus called himself an EU "dissident". I held up the Czech newspaper and basked in the glow of the dissidence for one cheap moment. That sounds silly, and it was. Later I understood that, at the time, I could bear staying in the European institutions by imagining being a well-disguised and sworn enemy of the real existing Europeism.

The political actions of the Czech president are another story; however, the man also wrote books. His essay "What is Europeism?" particularly inspired me. Klaus described "Europeism" as a "metaideology" consisting of "various post-democratic 'isms,' such as multiculturalism, feminism, ecologism, homosexualism, NGOism, etc." I looked around me; with the hosts of young female interns, this obvious half-Parliament in fact made up the very image of a meta-NGO.

At the accreditation desk I had already been received by a poster, which exhorted to saving the planet from a climate catastrophe. The initiator of the poster wasn't a party, but the European Parliament itself. This house knew neither government nor opposition; the four fractions of the People's Party, the Socialists, the Liberals and the Greens form an impervious mainstream regarding essential questions. Assuming that a representative didn't regard climate policy a parliamentary priority – was he thus a member of the opposition? An outlaw? A dissident?

I don't want to say anything against the female interns by the way. Their parties were namely not as wild as the old geezers claimed, but they constituted a particular unique tribe of the Eurocrat valley, the prettiest and also the most fleeting. A sound lingered in my ear, the voice of a Swiss girl who represented an NGO project focusing on Mexican children. She resorted to the word "slash" every chance she got when she spoke German with me. She called her work approach "realistic slash humanistic", and when she spoke about a guy she said "boy slash man". All of these small slashes, I thought, could also be a big Brusselian truth.

I also don't want to say anything against the Mickey Mouse bar. It was actually a much bigger, nicer and lighter place than the cafeteria in the Commission. More and more often, I went to the Mickey Mouse bar just to sit. I had many a glass of port with a southeastern Polish civil servant, thirty-three, who in his Christ-year started implementing an extensive guideline of a gender-neutral language. Out of "cleaning lady", Staszek had to make "cleaning staff", for "policemen" he said "police force". With his introverted shake of the head he took a look around. He said softly: "It's quite the ghetto, isn't it?"

Despite my hostile feelings, the nationalistic part of the political spectre didn't interest me. I wanted, on the contrary, to get to know those people who contemporaries called "Eurosceptics". I visited two leading representatives. In Prague, I met the leader of the SSO, a new political party formed in early 2009 surrounding Václav Klaus. In Brussels, I went to "Libertas", the then under construction Europe-list of the Irish businessman Declan Ganley.

Both places looked similar and smelled new. Both men had installed themselves in an expensive downtown location; both gazed lordly over the rooftops, one over the old town of Prague, the other over the Brusselian European Quarter. Both times I stood perplexed in front of electronic security access barriers: in Brussels in front of a "multiplexed digital system"; a doorbell with an operable scrolling text; in Kafka's hometown in front of a solid door without doorplate and a nameless blinking red light.

In Prague, Petr Mach received me, already leader of the party at the age of thirty-three, "Eurorealist", a model student of the sombre kind with parted hair. He said: "The European people are no demos." Democracy could therefore not work at European level. I asked him what kind of Europe he wanted. He argued for a reduced EU of governments, however mainly explained the weighting of votes in the Council, spoke of "depressive proportionality", demanded "better frameworks". The expressions sounded familiar to me. That he was, from the bottom of his heart, in favour of the elimination of the European Parliament I had to go to great lengths to drag out of him. First he wanted to run for this to-be eliminated Parliament.

In Brussels, Anita Kelly received me, also rather young, spokesperson for "Libertas". The gaunt Irish woman wanted to reduce the EU budget "sensibly"; the Czech had demanded ninety percent. Kelly had been an employee of the European Commission herself, but now she found that "laws shouldn't be made by people who aren't elected". She argued for democracy at European level with rather vague ideas. Amongst other things, she suggested that every Member State should elect their Commissioner directly. She hadn't yet formulated the thought of what a government composed by twenty-seven nationally elected Commissioners would be like.

I was left disillusioned. These Eurosceptics didn't think beyond the already existing institutions. They acted like Eurocrats and expressed themselves like Eurocrats. Not only was there no Europe that inspired to dream, but a shattering thought came over me: are all people dealing with institutional Europe cut from the same cloth? Are all of them – whether they agree or decline or criticise – made of paper and not of flesh?

There was nothing to be heard from Mach's party afterwards. "Libertas" wasn't even elected by the Irish into the European Parliament in 2009. The Monday after the lost European elections I saw Ms Kelly sit outside a "partner pub" to the snack bar "Maison Antoine". Partner pub meant that you got away with consuming brought-in chips. Exactly that was what one of the leading Eurosceptics was doing on the Monday after the lost election. She had spread out the brought chips on the café table. And was dipping them in sauce.

Chat by the Fire with the Congolese

As snow was falling in Brussels, I settled into the African quarter. I lived at the Estonian Eurocrat Tiina's place. While the Eurocrat, who herself didn't have any contact with her African neighbours, was visiting the exotic country of India, I savoured the exoticism of her African neighbourhood.

I was very excited about staying in this area. It was snowing when I arrived. A young African girl in leggings came out of a house and poured a bucket of hot water over her snow-covered French compact car. I recognised number 11 where I was to stay from a green shutter, which was always closed and covered the whole width of the house. The street was busy but the flat in the back was quiet. I stayed on the ground floor, and through a large antique window I could see a small walled garden. I was especially pleased with the fireplace. I had never been to Africa and never had mingled much with Africans, but the crackling fire and the snowy garden stirred up a fantasy in me. I named the fantasy "chat by the fire with the Congolese".

The African quarter is small; you can walk through it in ten minutes. It's called Matongé, after a place in the former Belgian colony of Congo, which was initially private property of the King and brutally tormented by Léopold II. About 4,000 Brusselians have Congolese roots.

I went to Matongé to recover. The African and the European quarter directly border each other; the divider is a clean cut. To the left of the rue du Trône office buildings are towering, the pavement is smoothed out for trolley cases. To the right of Trône there are narrow and low residential buildings, closely spaced, mostly quite austere looking, probably built for poor people. The pavement is bumpy.

It was like an African and a European kraal, side by side. As early as on my first expedition I learned that the parallels went even further. Just as the European community consisted of twenty-seven nations, just as the Congolese hadn't dominated Africa for a long time. Many in Matongé spoke better English than French and plenty were from Rwanda, in fact, numerous African nations were represented. I got to know a Tuareg from Niger, a Nigerian woman from Antwerp, a couple of Senegalese in "Le Dakar", Cameroonians and Burundians. Europe's proximity did however take its toll. Most Africans in Brussels no longer lived in Matongé; they only came there for the African services. The Eurocrats, like my Estonian landlady, had moved to Matongé and completely wrecked the rents.

When I was living in snowy Matongé, I wanted to experience Africa from morning to night. I wanted to have African breakfast. There didn't seem to be a proper African breakfast culture, the restaurants only opened around lunchtime. I also wanted to visit an African sauna. It didn't seem like there was a demand for that amongst the Africans. I found myself in a lukewarm sweat-chamber in the fitness club next door; they didn't even have cold showers.

I had a sauna alone with an Indian Sikh. The young Indian had been living in Brussels for a long time. He worked as a nurse but had another dream, namely becoming a Belgian police officer. "There you get a fixed salary even when you're not working." He said that he had a girlfriend in India; according to him the Moroccan women weren't faithful enough. He added that the Belgian women didn't appeal to him. "As a nurse I often see that they have black spots on their skin." I looked at him in astonishment. He tapped with his finger on his face to illustrate. "Yes, the Belgian women have tiny little black spots, everywhere."

The greatest day experience was the "Passage d'Ixelles", an old and grey shopping arcade with two dozen hair salons, and stores everywhere with artificial hair and packages with pre-braided human hair. On Saturdays the salons were full, mostly with waiting and gossiping costumers, the hair cult could truly keep the African women captivated all day long.

The hairdressers worked behind glass. I found it difficult to understand what was going on. One woman had white mousse put in her frilled hair out of a plastic tube. Behind another pane sat a skinny black princess, slightly bent forward. She had a white towel over her shoulders; heavy, long locks were hanging over her face. She sat there without moving; her eyes were covered. The hairdresser had a big needle and was sewing with vigour into the customer's head. Did I see right, was she actually sewing into that woman's scalp? Maybe that wasn't a woman after all, was I looking at a doll? Suddenly the supposed doll raised its head and the princess looked at me baring her white pupils. Someone called out to me from a men's hair salon: "Would you like a haircut?" I took off.

The following days I looked at the women on the streets differently. If I saw an African girl I would automatically ask myself if she had sewn-on hair. Suddenly, it hit me that literally no African woman wore her hair naturally; most of them wore it straight. If I saw a white Belgian girl I couldn't help myself but to compulsively look for black spots on her skin. I don't know where the Indian man looks, but the Belgian women that I saw were flawlessly beautiful.

The greatest night experience was first of all "Le Président". The chic restaurant and dancing bar, lit only by thin red stripe lights and red liquor ads, attracted men of presidential figures, one old and one young, clad in their finest suits. If they hadn't both been drinking alone, they could have passed as African opposition politicians, biding their time in the Brusselian winter.

Secondly, I frequently hung out in "La Callebasse", a cramped bar in the narrow angle of a corner house; exclusively Congolese. In the beginning I used my bar changes to feed the fire in the open fireplace at home. To tell the truth, the chimney smoked terribly. The European Carrie Bradshaw, who now finally believed herself to be in the realm of senses, exuded the aroma of bacon. One female European guest even refused to stay, saying: "I'll get smoke poisoning here." I secretly buried the idea of a chat by the fire with the Congolese.

Instead something similar happened in "La Callebasse". Later on I fled there often, more often with Staszek. It wasn't easy for Staszek that there were so few women present, we just sat there and decently watched the Cameroonian waitress Danielle from afar. I got the impression that the Polish bachelor liked Danielle. I became more confident. I didn't understand why he always took out Flemish or English girls to dinner anyway. Danielle spoke French with a deep, husky accent. I really liked the way she held up her chin when she was accepting tips.

On my first visit I was still alone. I saw a young Nubian woman sitting there in the "Callebasse" between two sweetly smiling Belgian gentlemen. One of the men disappeared; the other was her husband. The Nubian woman waved me over to their table. She was a proud woman; her posture alone spoke of unaffected pride. She warned me about African women who throw themselves at white men. She then prophesied with a knowing look: "Once you go black, you never go back."

The owner of the bar told me that, by all means, even female Eurocrats ended up in his Congolese men's bar.

I asked him if he didn't find this breed from the European institutions boring. "Bored, rather", he answered. He became more precise. A couple of days before, a female Flemish Commission official had come in, good-looking and in her thirties. "She wanted coke and an African", he explained, "and at the same time." He did have African men, but not the cocaine, so she left just as quickly. The owner couldn't have imagined how much courage his nice little story had instilled in me. The next day I wandered back to the European kraal in a much lighter manner.

Studio Europe

"Carousel, carousel", the Eurovision song goes, "spin quick and well, quick and well." Life in a central quarter of Brussels has been spinning for many years, "and outside the world flashes by".

The world, a streetwalker district in the residential area Alhambra, next to the Flemish theatre. The neighbourhood ranged from Flemish, to Albanian, to Moroccan; the prostitutes mostly Bulgarian and the suitors mostly Turkish and Arab, besides a house with illegal transsexual immigrants from Ecuador. The "carousel", a constant rotation of up to eight hundred cars crawling by every hour, was being tackled by a citizen initiative called "Comité Alhambra" since 1999. In the beginning of 2009, the local authorities hammered pegs into the street. Before the carousel was blocked, I spun with it.

It all began with me ending up with a "Comité Alhambra" petition in my hands. The Comité kept the names of its members classified and the meetings took place in secret. A particular clause in the petition caught my attention, a complaint about "aggressive transsexuals". I didn't know anything about transsexuals. Aggressive transsexuals seemed worth a visit even more.

I went to Alhambra by day. I spoke to three members of the Comité. They had thirty to forty members, many of whom were Flemish and citizens of the free West; the Albanian and Moroccan neighbours were not represented. The Comité had gone on an excursion. There's "more social control" in Antwerp, one of them told me, compared to the Brusselian "laisser-faire mentality". Another one called for a "centre for the poor women" like in Antwerp.

A veteran Comité campaigner had moved to Alhambra in 1984. "It was quiet, it was calm", she said, "the kids were playing in the streets." It turned out that in the match "residents against street walkers", the facet "EU against EU" was concealed. The veteran had been interpreter, mainly working for the EU. It particularly bothered her that one of the hotels by the hour was actually run by a female Commission official. The hotel by the hour had a very fitting name; "Studio Europe".

The Commission official, whom I could no longer find in the Commission, used to be quite "plain". "Wears a suit and not too much make-up." She had once in 2004 burst into a Comité meeting and "made quite the racket". The veteran said that she felt threatened. A seventy year-old toothless Belgian "original whore" had shouted "Gestapo" at her. "Just because I'm German."

I went to Alhambra by night. I lived there for a couple of days, bedstead number 13, the flat of an interpreter who was out of town, who had bought the place in rue de Commerçants hoping for an upvaluation of the central quarter. On the other end of the street there was a café where you could get a bowl of hot soup even late at night amongst prostitutes of unknown gender looking to recover.

Carousel, carousel, I could see it spinning out there on the boulevard from the Turkish-Bulgarian corner bar. There were men in the "Tropicana", and prostitutes came in to get warm. I was introduced to Dschingis at the bar, the Turkish owner. He wore his shirt wide-open, his upperbody and arms were ever vibrantly moving. As we were speaking, his azure eyes pierced me with attentive devotion. His gaze abruptly changed when he turned it to his bar, then he furrowed his brow in suspicion.

And suddenly, the first transsexual of my life stood next to me. Sofia from Spain, tall with broad shoulders and sad eyes under a crust of make-up. She softly stroked my face with her hand and complimented my skin as soft and nice. She suggested going to a hotel by the hour. Fifty euros, she declared gently. For seven thousand euros she had had a vagina made so that she could experience "phantasms" but "no orgasms". I could only think of stupid questions to ask her. After five minutes, Sofia gave up the seduction and returned to the street.

The aggression of the transsexuals was only vaguely accounted for by the Comité Alhambra. Rumour had it that there was a fight with transsexual participation a couple of years earlier. One member expressed himself slightly more carefully: "The transvestites are simply loud." From

February 2009, the cars could no longer spin, but the prostitution mill keeps on grinding in Alhambra. "Carousel, carousel, spin quick and well, quick and well, and take care that no one falls off."

Nocturne

That night I wanted to go to bed early. That I was still staggering through Brussels the following morning was because of the Huguenot. He had an ordinary German first name and unusually nice-sounding French family names. Quite simply, a Huguenot.

We were only meeting for a Thai food dinner; however, he took me into the most intoxicating depths of the African splendour of Brussels. That night confused me. Let's see if I can remember at all.

The Huguenot had the delicately chiselled features of a gentleman; the abundance of his midriff was well proportioned. The staidness of his Alemannic accent was deceiving; he was agile like a panther.

The Huguenot was an international, he organised the division of European money. He had been to Iraq, in Bagdad's "Green Zone"; even when he had gone to pee there was a British soldier guarding the toilet door. He had been to the Balkans, to Papua New Guinea. The EU relies on external firms during such engagements as well.

The Huguenot called his firm a "Facility". I learnt that the Council of Europe had a bank and that this bank financed prisons on the Western Balkans. I further learnt that the EU had donated one billion dollars to Iraq, however didn't hand it out themselves, but as a precaution, let the World Bank and the UN take over. I didn't pick up on any evidence for corruption. Whenever the Huguenot mentioned the Facility, he expressed himself with honesty and accurate severity.

When I think about this night I almost only remember smells. The bodies and spaces of the Valley of the Eurocrats don't remind me of any smells, at best they remind me of the memorable phrase of a civil servant married to a Commission secretary: "I don't know a neater person than my wife."

After midnight, the Huguenot took me to his spots. Those weren't spots for Eurocrats, but rather for a young, elegant and sexually aware nobility of the night, for styled African queens and confident black princes with glittering golden Cartier cuff links on their white shirts. We drank cognac out of balloons that became bigger every time.

In the peak of the night, we steered towards the club "144", to the lone summit of Beauté. "They have a triple 'face control' over there", the Huguenot warned me, "you can't always get in." In between the three control points there were long corridors, we passed the first and the second gates without any difficulty. The third bouncer, at the very entrance of the club, shot a sharply accentuated "Bonsoir" at me. I jerked. He let me in.

The Huguenot knew how to party on the cheap, and ordered a bottle of vodka. Perhaps that's why I only remember scents from that night. Two metres away someone was smoking a cigar. For a long time I couldn't even sense it, so overpowering were the perfumes and the odours of the room and bodies. These smells were strange to me. I couldn't see any plants, but heavy drops sloshed over me like a cool tropical rain dripping from flower sepals. To sense, to believe, to dream; that is Brussels as well.

When we stepped into the street it was light. Two women spoke to us and I heard the word "massage". How do I free myself from these prostitutes, I thought to myself, then followed the still jolly Huguenot. The four of us got into a taxi.

We landed in front of a door, on which it said: "Le privée". Inside people were dancing, it didn't look anything like a bordello, and suddenly the Maghrebian masseuses ignored us. They had probably just needed a lift. I stared dimwittedly at the dance floor. My eyes started to droop and the Huguenot poked me awake. When he let me go it was almost nine o'clock.

After that, the Huguenot flew away; the Facility needed him in Sarajevo. While I remember in confusion, the shower is running next door. Once again I'm living at a Eurocrat's place, once again this Eurocrat is taking remarkably long showers. These Eurocrats, they all shower themselves into oblivion.

The Rocco Case

I wanted to reconstruct a key moment in the history of the European Union. I researched for a long time. Even longer still I pondered how to present the results of my research.

I was afraid I would have to put forward a list of imposed assertions, such as: No, I don't have anything against gays! Yes, I've been friends with gays! But of course, I'm against any kind of discrimination!

Someone who begins a story like that soon arouses suspicion. I have to live with that. I will try to mention my own prejudices as well. They have repeatedly changed throughout the course of my research. What didn't change was the feeling I invariably had during the reconstruction: still it was right to come to this place. Fundamental things were negotiated in Brussels.

The Rocco Buttiglione case had intrigued me for a long time. Never before had a designated Commissioner been removed from power. After the hearing in the "Committee on Civil Liberties, Justice and Home Affairs" of the European Parliament, twenty-seven members voted against Buttiglione and twenty-six in his favour. This was celebrated in 2004 as a triumph for the homosexual movement.

In the beginning of my reconstruction I had the following belief: a religious Catholic wasn't allowed to become a Commissioner for the EU since he represented the Bible's and the Catholic Church's opinion on homosexuality. I found that disagreeable inasmuch as Buttiglione seemed to be the most qualified of all candidates. He was fluent in the six most common languages of the EU plus Portuguese, he could have communicated with three quarters of the Union citizens in their mother tongues. The fact that the philosophy professor was a European Minister in Berlusconi's cabinet was perhaps no recommendation. The fact that he was a friend and advisor of Pope John Paul II; that, I saw as a reference.

I contacted ILGA-Europe, the European governing body of homosexual lobbies. Within a short time, I managed to set up a meeting with the woman who had coordinated the campaign against Buttiglione in Brussels. She had switched to Amnesty International in the meantime. At the end of a workday I picked her up from her new job. Amnesty was situated in the heart of the European Quarter, with a wonderful view. You have found somewhere pretty with my donations, I thought to myself.

Christine Loudes was French. She was about forty, and I would describe her clothes as tame and understated late-hippie style, with loose trousers. She had soft features and a soft gait, and reminded me of a woman I had almost married once.

We walked through the hell of rush-hour traffic to a rather unremarkable café of her choice. As we were walking we already started talking about the topic in question. Oh dear, I thought to myself, Ms Loudes will not be happy about my text afterwards. Suddenly she interrupted the conversation and turned to a blind man who stood lost at a zebra crossing on rue Belliard. She exchanged a couple of words with him and helped him find his way. I hadn't even noticed the blind man. Oh dear, I thought to myself, I am dealing with a really good person.

"It was my first year in Brussels", she told me in the café, "it was really exciting." Unravelling before me was the story of a little girl, who completely unexpectedly overthrew a sinister and powerful man. It was hard not to sympathise with her story.

She described the proceedings of the campaign as follows: ILGA-Europe had acquired a collection of Buttiglione's homophobic statements from the Italian association "Arcigay". The founding of the "Intergroup" for homosexual matters had already been promoted, and a list of gay-friendly committee members had been formulated.

Ms Loudes had herself listened in on the hearing. She said that Buttiglione had behaved "annoyingly". He had made further "homophobic remarks" during the hearing. She couldn't remember any of these remarks.

Later during the conversation there was an irritating moment. I posed the insignificant question whether the lobbyists of the homosexual lobby are homosexuals. "We don't enquire about sexual orientation", Ms Loudes responded. And to that she added in a general tone: "You aren't allowed to ask, you might get sued."

After this instruction I took heed not to ask Ms Loudes about her own sexual orientation. I probably wouldn't have asked her anyway, but still a small shadow of restraint started to lower itself over our small coffee table. And I had just proved myself eager to learn. We talked – as was right and proper in the spring season of '09 – not about homosexuals, but about "LGBT people" with "LGBT rights".

Next, I went to the Greens fraction of the European Parliament. While walking through the Greens' long hallways, I got a foreboding of why they loved the half-Parliament so much and why they, as the only political family, always sent their best to Brussels. The best are well deployed in the capital, since environmental issues are strongly Europeanised and active groups can achieve disproportionately high leverage despite limited support. The Greens' hallways were one large gallery of applied NGOism. I walked along an exuberant collection of hundreds and hundreds of posters, which shouted out everything that was harmful to the world. Hardly any of these posters, one of them an image of the Indian caste system, had anything to do with the European Parliament's authorities.

I visited one of the representatives who received Buttiglione's quotes in 2004, the Dutch Green Kathalijne Buitenweg. As before, I managed to set up a meeting with this LGBT advocate in no time at all. I was her first appointment for the day, and the brusque, curly redhead in her late thirties received me with a healthy freshness. The Dutch woman said that she was surprised by the outcome of the campaign as well: "I thought we were going to lose." She had at most expected an exchange of responsibilities. Buttiglione was nominated for "Justice, Freedom and Security", an office, which, according to Ms Buitenweg, should "promote anti-discrimination". "I would be okay with him being the Commissioner of Fisheries."

I asked ILGA and Arcigay for the collection of quotes, and after many requests and many weeks of waiting I finally got a hold of them. Reading through the two pages I understood why they had let me wait for so long. I couldn't find anything offensive. Was I that coarse; was I a homophobe myself? I asked the LGBT people if this paper was all there was. They said yes.

I read the paper over and over. Buttiglione did constitute homosexuality a sin, however he called this moral judgement politically irrelevant. He called himself a sinner and stressed that sins are no cases for courts. "If all immoral acts were punished by law, there'd be few people left walking free on the street, we'd all be in jail." The paper contained Buttiglione's proposition to support women financially so that they would refrain from abortion. I was agonising over this. I couldn't wrap my head around who was discriminated against by this statement.

I wanted to hear the other side. There had been Catholic representatives from Poland present during the hearing, and one of them had defended Buttiglione. I wrote to this representative, repeatedly, and in several different languages. I actually proposed coming to Poland. Not even a reply was sent my way. Well, I thought, half of the population of the European Union are heterosexual Catholics – who lobbies for them?

Towards the end, I watched a recording of this hearing which had been subject to many a discussion. The tribunal lasted over three hours, and the interpreters had left towards the end. There were many different topics, but still the representatives of Intergroup took to the floor in accurately timed intervals. They fired questions at Buttiglione, and every time they took their claims to a higher level. The Dutch Buitenweg asked him about sin. The English actor Cashman, famous for the first gay kiss in TV-soap history, expressed his "deep dismay" over the accused party. When Buttiglione replied to him, Cashman shook his head with lips quivering with anger. The left-liberal Dutch In't Veld demanded for a "pro-active" development of the LGBT rights.

Buttiglione replied calmly and ingeniously. He quoted Kant, Max Weber, Cicero, polished in five languages and asserted his preference of anti-discrimination. Even scrutinising the hearing closely, I couldn't detect any homophobic expressions. I could say that the LGBT lobbyist with the soft gait had lied to my face. I want to summarise it more gently: presumably, Ms Loudes' recollection of her memories was completely based on emotions.

"Things have changed significantly since then", Buitenweg summed up the period of the European Parliament ending in 2009. The Dutch Green should be proved right. That was revealed in the last Strasbourg sitting of the parliament period of 2004–2009, when the Dutch left-liberal In't Veld took her next swipe.

She proposed an amendment to the Human Right's Report in which the Pope would be "strongly condemned" because of his position on condoms. This time, it fell through. 253 representatives voted against it, however 199 would have liked to accuse the Pope in the same breath as dictators. Things have changed since the Rocco case. The LGBT lobby has improved itself. Since 2004, they have doubled their number of personnel in Brussels.

The Hunters

Once, I was going around with the hunters. First, I visited the house of the hunters' lobby in Brussels, secondly, they taught me how to shoot in Flanders, and thirdly, they told me a nasty Dutch story.

After at least one Dutch woman had struck me as unpleasant, I immediately believed the nasty Dutch story. Admittedly: to begin with it was just a story, it wasn't proven. In the Netherlands, the story began, hunting is largely restricted. For this reason, there had been uncontrolled breeding of geese, the masses had caused considerable damage. The following solution had thus been found: "In Holland, geese are now gassed to death."

I found the house of the hunters' association FACE in a poor Brusselian residential area, a fifteen minute walk from the office fortresses of the European Quarter. FACE represented seven million European hunters; the environmental lobbies afforded better locations. In the one bigger office space, which had been constructed at the expense of the little garden, I was introduced to young employees who spoke and wrote and looked exactly like the employees of environmental protection associations.

The rest of the building, entwining over several floors in narrow nooks and crannies, felt like a hunter's cabin. Many small antlers hung on the walls. A stuffed bustard was placed in a glass cabinet, the largest bird able to fly, with a silly white beard. A stuffed fox was lying on top of a cupboard in the storeroom. The ones who grin so viciously even in death, deserve this fate, I decided spontaneously.

Christine Rödlach led me through the building, a beautiful Tyrolean of pleasantly relaxed nature, at FACE for nine months. Before that she had been an office manager to a Christian Democrat representative in the European Parliament. She had just acquired her hunting licence and had already shot a Tyrolean chamois. She was about to get married to a hunting Tyrolean civil servant working for the European Council.

Wild animals are not the EU's responsibility, said Rödlach. I asked why the hunters then needed a lobby in Brussels. "The EU is trying to create regulations via detours", she replied, "because of pressure from the environmental lobbies."

She gave me an example, "trade in seal products", a draft regulation by the Commissioner for the Environment. Seal hunting is in fact marginal in Europe, only in Finland and Sweden is it allowed to shoot a couple of hundred seals. The Commissioner for the Environment's biggest argument, however, was "public concern". I started to understand the rise of the lobbies with that small example: animal rights activists campaign against seal hunting, the media shows brutal pictures from Canada. A Commissioner is looking for popularity, brings the issue via the seal hunting detour to EU level, and all interest groups involved send additional personnel to Brussels.

The next Sunday, the hunters took me clay pigeon shooting with them in Flanders. I proved to be completely clueless. The Flemish shooting range was situated at the bottom of a semi-circular slope covered with bright orange things. I was painstakingly slow to realise that these orange discs were in fact the clay pigeons. Steered by remote control, they flew out of a small wooden shed.

Practice makes perfect, the relaxed Tyrolean girl explained. The more precise the hunter shoots, the less the prey suffers. The other members participating in the excursion: her fiancé, two female journalists, a bank lobbyist and the German wife of the CEO of FACE, who was a white African and also a falconer. Most of them had at least one piece of green clothing on them; the local Flemish hunters were significantly greener. A hyperactive Spaniard – formerly with FACE, now a consultant – explained the usage of the gun. He explained that, according to Belgian regulation, the gun has to be pointed down while being loaded.

And then I had to shoot. How did it feel? I could get used to the smell, the shot itself felt like a blow to the shoulder. I wasn't even close to a hit. That's no fun.

Towards the end of my huntsman career, I enquired about Holland. The nasty story was confirmed; during the summer thousands of grey geese had been gassed to death with CO_2. The traditional goose hunt had however already been re-established. And it was said that, since the gassing, the Dutch knew how to appreciate their hunters again.

The Directory

I never needed anything as much in Brussels as this book. Once I was having lunch with a French interpreter, when she suddenly lowered her voice. She had spotted the leading participants from the conference where she was interpreting sitting at the next table. The conference was about liberalisation of the postal services.

The civil servants, who were flown in from different Member States, would mostly remain silent, the interpreter told me. During conferences at this level there were only a couple languages being interpreted, and the eastern European civil servants' English was useless, so they kept rather quiet. She thought it better when they did: "Personally, I would rather not have them come at all."

The interpreter pointed out a man at the next table to me. He had a thin, bald head. He was the manager for the international consultant agency PriceWaterhouseCoopers. "He sets the tone at the conference", the interpreter said. From this point on I examined the older gentleman properly. I finally had the feeling that I had laid my eyes on a truly powerful man. This was a rare feeling in Brussels; essentially the hierarchies appear to be flat on the surface. Since it's impossible to have an overview of who is how important in which Member State, it was better just to be polite to everyone.

I observed the consultant closely. He had a piercing stare. When he was spoken to, he stopped his fork with the piece of speared meat mid-air. His answer was brief and he then went back to chewing the meat intensely.

Up until then I had no idea. The importance of the "Big Four", it was completely new to me. I also didn't know that every European Commission programme must be evaluated externally, a business which nurtures a whole commuting belt of consultants and, in turn, the "Big Four". I had come to Brussels quite naïve. I didn't even know that the Commission subsidised environmental lobbies, such as the World Wildlife Fund.

The work of the environmental lobby could easily be observed. One grey winter day, the Council of Finance Ministers was deliberating about the support of major banks – the "bail-out" – while female Greenpeace activists, under a banner saying "Bail out the climate!" were blocking the entrance to the Council building. Barely anyone paid them attention. I noted the routine and perfect preparation of all participants. Two activists had chained themselves to the metal fence, the police had already brought the proper hacksaws, the NGO cameramen had obtained the best possible shooting spots. One pretty activist, freed from her chains, was carried to a police van while arching her naked navel area. I found that quite erotic, it even caught the cameraman's attention. I asked myself: am I really watching a demonstration, or rather the filming of an eco-porn film?

In cases of doubt of any kind I now had this book, "The European Public Affairs Directory". The most extensive directory of lobbies and institutions in Brussels, 578 pages, large format, high-gloss paper, weighing exactly two kilos. The 2009 edition contained 3,500 lobbies, 7,000 lobbyists and 20,000 people working with European affairs. It was published by DODS in London, print and online, both for a very steep price. For five months I had begged for a copy, and then finally it was delivered in a big, white and well-wrapped bag from the Swiss Post. Since then, I only very reluctantly left the house without my Directory.

I was constantly flipping through the Directory's pages. Already the foreword swept me off to far-away galaxies. Three thousand regulations, the editor wrote, are annually being transcribed and filed "under Comitology". The editor carefully added that: "From now on it will be impossible to claim any influence in Brussels without a perfect mastery of Comitology."

For a long time I was astonished by the fact that a myriad of young people in the Eurocrat valley were telling me the same story: "I work for a company that's creating websites for the Commission." One of these externalised propagandists was working for a Danish company producing short online films, which in turn also needed the production of an audience. Thus, "European Service

Network" made twenty-one video animations for the environmental Commissioner's website. Twenty-one climate friendly teenagers frolicked through the frame and suggested measures to prevent climate change in twenty-one languages. The German youngster recommended: "I collect corks and give them to a company, and then they're recycled into sandals. They're super comfortable and environmental-friendly, why don't you buy a pair too!"

However, also available online was a "Financial Transparency System" of the European Commission. There I learned that "European Service Network" had earned 5,299,043 euros in 2007 from the Commission. I looked for this company in the Directory, but couldn't find it. Even though they employed a hundred people in Brussels. Good heavens, I thought, there is so much going on in Gotham City that not even the Directory knows it all!

I absolutely loved wandering about with the blue book. Preferably, I would have liked to read from it whole theatre nights long. How melodious some of the agencies' names sounded! "Electus", "Brattle Group", "Inside Consulting", "Métaphore", "Plato Communications", "Political Intelligence", "Sovereign Strategy".

And who, if not all, kept an office in the capital! The "Centre Européen des Silicones", the "European Animal Protein Association", the "Water Metre Producers", the "Breakfast Cereal Association", the parquet manufacturers, the resin producers, the parquet importers, the "European Egg Processors Association", the "European

Smokeless Tobacco Council", the "European Committee of Professional Diving Instructors". I was motivated, I was inspired, I was moving on to new pastures. The lists in the Directory were indeed the true poetry of Brussels.

Publisher's note: Since January 2011 a new, comprehensive directory is available: stakeholder.eu

Lost Sectors

I was cheerfully getting into the Brusselian Métro, suddenly my shoulder bag was gone. I don't want to recount all the things that were in the bag, else I might start crying instead of writing. The account for my visits to different sector lobbies can be added to my losses. The landowners' organisation, the seed association, the maize millers; everything was gone.

I had gazed at the biodiversity of the Eurocrat valley as if electrified. The editors of the Directory themselves wrote that there are at least twice as many lobbyists as the seven thousand listed by them. A larger amount of these highly communicative people deputises sector interests. I had made appointments with some of them.

I started with the chemical association CEFIC, which keeps a building complex with numerous wings in southern Brussels, and a hundred and fifty employees. I was told the story of the chemical regulation "Reach". About two hundred people – delegates, assistants, consultants, civil servants, industrial and environmental lobbyists – had founded a travelling circus for many years, in which they didn't work on anything else but "Reach". Later on, I knocked on the doors of the smaller sectors; the manufacturers of cement, liquor, private wagons, lifts, and the whey producers. Every single one represented about ten thousand positions. Having had my notes stolen, I had to think of a way to remember, without the numbers, names and quotes.

I'm afraid I have completely forgotten my visit to the landowners. The "European Landowners", I had envisioned them glorious, either rural or mundane, maybe wearing breeches; however a middle-aged French solicitor escorted me into a clean conference room. The French woman cordially shared her information with me, however her speech about sustainability quickly went in one ear and out the other. I don't wish for the thief of my shoulder bag to suffer agonies. He shall only read my notes from this interview, from beginning to end. That would be punishment enough.

In the seed association's conference room, I was brushed by one of the biggest values' debates of our time. The general secretary of "Euroseeds" spoke with considerable affection of "GMO": genetically modified organisms. He found it interesting that Polish conservatives and Italian communists are united in their dismissal of GMOs, their Catholic background really shines through. He emphasised the small importance of his sector; the major American GMO company was making about as much profit as a mid-sized electronics store. He himself was a blond German, squared, lean, agile, elegant. He had already "tasted blood" in Brussels decades ago, but introduced himself as a cultivator from Lower Saxony. His German was riddled with Anglicisms. I eagerly took note of his globalised jargon. That is something only a Brusselian thief will now have the pleasure to enjoy.

The loss of the account from my maize miller-visit hurts the most. The general secretary of "Maize Millers" had been suspicious to my request for a visit; she only invited me after the submission of many assertions. However, she completely won me over inside her clean conference room.

The general secretary of the Maize Millers was from south Italy. She was young and short, pretty and feisty, had pleasant curves and a passion for food. She had written a book on "food law". The framework of guidelines in Europe, she had found out, is equivalent to religion in other cultures. She enthused about white maize, about its scent. There was a see-through box in her office, containing maize in different phases of grinding process. I smelled it. She explained that the maize was too old to give off any scent. She was right.

The Italian woman hadn't been in Brussels for very long. I wasn't allowed to write anything about what she said concerning the topic "GMO" anyway, so I steered the conversation to more general topics. I said that I barely knew any Italians in Brussels and had never been invited to an Italian reception. She said that she would introduce me to some Italians and prove to me how "crazy" her countrymen could be. That sounded tempting, unfortunately we lost touch afterwards. Only then did it hit me that the clever maize miller would have been something for Staszek.

I also talked to her about Brussels. The curvy Italian described the place of our landing without mercy: "Brussels smells like nothing." I objected to that, maybe that lack of scent could only be applied to the European Quarter. She was very convinced though. She had lived in Cairo and said that even the Arabian corners of Brussels smelled like nothing. Not even like the Orient, simply of nothing at all.

That was the thought that stayed in my head. A capital for five hundred million people – that smells like nothing? This is why, dear thief, I don't need my notebook back. I now walked through Brussels much more uplifted. Uplifted, and sniffing.

The Security

It has always been said that Brussels is a dangerous city. I didn't want to believe that at first and assumed that the Eurocrats were the ones behind that bad reputation. Staszek told me once: "Eurocrats go where they feel safe, to their 'comfort zone'. But does that make them happy? Does that make me happy?"

From the life stories of the European bubble, I acquired the image of a kind of people treated with kid gloves all their lives. If now such sheltered citizens make for five percent of a city of a million people and earn three times as much as the locals, then they feel threatened.

As I had lost my shoulder bag, I looked at this in a much more differentiated way. My notes from the visit at "Securitas" were also gone. If the city hadn't been so unsafe, I thought, I would have been able to describe the work of the security services to my readers. From the manager I had learned that "Securitas" alone provided about a thousand guards for the European institutions. Only one out of eleven applicants was hired, "we examine the applicant's life very thoroughly". If your brother owns a disco, you already have a problem. The manager showed me the training centre. There, the guards learned "how to look at things". I can't tell you anything more without my notes.

I wanted to know how dangerous Brussels actually is, and got a hold of the figures. I rummaged through the criminal statistics of the Brusselian police. I read that between the years of 2000 and 2008 defamation and vandalism increased, offences such as "demolition" however regressed. For fewer stolen cars, more bikes were being nicked instead. Murder, discrimination and burglary stagnated. The statistics seemed quite reassuring. Or were they suspiciously stable? The total number of offences stayed the same over the years.

I created my own survey. I chose twelve people from the European bubble, reasonably representative, each of them from a different European country. My sole interest was what had happened to them personally, no rumours. I promised them anonymity.

The good news was that four out of the twelve people asked hadn't fallen victims to any crimes. The remaining eight had something to report. "During my five years in Brussels I didn't once feel threatened", one of them told me. "I have only been subject to criminal activities three times. For example my bike, which I had bought right after my arrival at the market for stolen bikes, was nicked after three weeks from the bike parking outside the European Parliament. Three years ago, my neighbour at that time (dealer and drug consumer, no foreign background) stole a laptop and a digital camera from my flat as well as some books from the attic. I therefore feel rather safe in Brussels. I often go jogging in the dark unlit Josaphat Park and only feel slightly anxious at times, and that is because of the iPhone worth five hundred and fifty euros that I use for listening to music." Two other people reported on having had their laptops stolen, "at the Gare Centrale", "my first flat got broken into; unfortunately I wasn't insured against burglary".

One woman had once been accompanied to her house at night. As soon as her company had left, "two guys appeared behind me and shouted the typical salutation, 'ça va?' They pestered me with questions, if I was living alone or if someone was waiting for me in the flat." The woman only managed to escape the men by running towards a car some stranger was parking. Another woman told me that a man had pushed her to the side on the pavement: "He introduced himself as Sajid from Syria and shouted 'Kiss!'"

Victims six to eight reported: "Fortunately nothing really bad has happened to me, only the windows to my car were broken three times, but they never took anything." – "Only once did someone try to snatch my handbag in the Parc du Cinquantenaire (in November around six o'clock), but without success." – "Once, bike was taken by two stoned Belgians and thus ended up in a fully unexpected fight; one attempted robbery one evening; no trust at all in the Brussels police's capability."

I rummaged even deeper into the statistics of the Brussels police department, seventy-two pages long. On page seventy-one, in "Appendix 4", I noticed something. The heading "lost property" revealed an increase of downright Soviet method. In 2000, less than 4,000 pieces of property had been lost, in 2008 more than 52,000. There it was, black on white, why the Eurocrats experienced an unreasonable sense of anxiety. People just lose things easily. Twelve times easier than before.

The Tobacco Lobby

Since we stopped believing in Satan, the entertainment business now produces other embodiments of evil for us. The character "tobacco lobbyist" is one of them. On one of the countless Brusselian spring days, with their cold, grey and cloudy skies blocking out any kind of spring feelings, one of these guys opened his door for me. Let me start by saying that barely anyone in Brussels had been that pleasant to me.

It's said that, after Washington, Brussels is the place with the most lobbyists in the world. The definition of lobbyism is already highly political. Are we allowed to call the full-time Jacobins of climate politics this? If someone slips me his business card during the lunch buffet of an integration conference, which reads: "The climate is changing, are you?" – was I not lobbied right there?

The smallest definition problem is caused by consultants that let themselves be hired by anyone who's willing to pay. They're very discreet. I kept striving to get interviews but most of the time they didn't respond. "Value Added Europe" informed me, they "didn't really work in European Public Affairs", they were "building warehouses".

I was all the more amazed when one of them actually sat in front of me in "Pleon" on avenue des Arts. Already in his first response did he call himself "for sale" and rejected sugar-coated job descriptions such as "advocacy". He said that he had never refused a single client. His pain threshold was high, "I wouldn't want to sell rockets". One of his clients was the tobacco company BAT.

Hermann Drummer, in his fifties, smooth grey hair, dark suit, dark polo shirt. The Frank received me in a see-through conference room, in the middle of the corridor. Through the glass one could see attractive female employees walking by. There was a young blonde sitting at the table as well, new to the company. She was listening the whole time, with a constant expression of amusement spread across her sensual lips. She was, to my slight disappointment, constantly gazing at her boss.

I posed the only interesting question. The tobacco industry was under fire, Europe was covered with smoking bans, a company like Philip Morris was even paying some kind of protection money to the EU, of 1.25 billion. In addition the satanic image of the profession. So I asked the tobacco lobbyist if he didn't want to be loved. Drummer answered very quickly: "I am loved, I know it, not just by my wife." He instantly uttered more gently: "I experience true appreciation." At times something timid flitted across his eyes and added to his humorous and youthful grin. I believed him to be loved by women.

In truth, we spoke very little about tobacco. I was the cause of that; the highly educated political scientist had had some of my dream jobs, I was bursting with curiosity. As a journalist, he had written about "wine, travel, hotels" in Switzerland, had earned many francs for little work. He had been a speechwriter for a top politician, who later became the President of Germany, Johannes Rau. "I have never complained about my life", the fortunate recounted.

Drummer was at the moment working for "British American Tobacco" on a campaign against cigarette smuggling. I told him to keep in mind that he could also lose the hearts of the smokers that way. Weren't the smokers around the border areas the biggest smugglers? Wasn't cigarette smuggling boosting European integration? He explained that the campaign was about something else, about truckloads from China and the Ukraine. I did however see that he immediately processed this relevant piece of information I had given him.

The SPD member also explained to me what lobbyists actually do. He did a lot of "comitology"; he let me in on this secret doctrine. He liked the European Parliament since he could wander about in there freely. He liked the alleged meat market at place Lux; to Drummer a unique European ambience, but to Staszek only a reason for tormented exclamations such as: "The weather is really depressing here, pitch-black clouds, wind and rain, and very deep in the Eurocrat valley on top of everything!"

When the skies above Brussels finally bestowed something that felt like a spring feeling upon us, I let the trusted tobacco lobbyist extend an invitation to place Lux for a glass of wine. You would think that the old cheeky devil had gotten to me. However me, I was only enjoying the observation of a truly happy life.

Facebook

The moment I want to mock Facebook, I am caught off guard by an in memoriam notice. My English translator is dead. Next to his picture are a couple verses by the deceased. He wrote them shortly before his death, and he published them on Facebook. Suddenly, the shadow of death falls upon my subject.

In 2009, Facebook was a madly growing online network. Two hundred million people interacted with each other, shared personal photos, gathered friendships. I knew someone who had two thousands "friends" there. Facebook disgusted me from the very beginning. However, in the fleeting passing-by environment of the European bubble, the platform was very big. "Are you on Facebook?" could be heard from all directions. Every week there were parties in Brussels that you wouldn't even know about if you weren't on Facebook.

Once I had a really good night out in a bar. "Delecta" was a deli from the fifties, where unusually beautiful women diffused an atmosphere of unfathomable bisexuality. I had been brought there by a Belgian artiste, who was haunted by an alternative city map. It was a really good night. The barkeeper, a sexually aware and cryptically smiling woman, said to Alessia: "Tu as l'air d'avoir de beaux seins." That was a French compliment, any kind of translation would sound crude, "beaux seins" means "nice breasts". The crackling electric charge in the air faded away when another Belgian girl from our group came across one of her Facebook friends. She had never seen the man before. An excruciating minute passed by, embarrassing, irritated, confounded. Rather two thousand enemies, I swore to myself, than one single Facebook friend.

Completely biased, I went to a debate held in the European Parliament, called "Communicating through Facebook – yes or no?" It was organised by Hêbê, a young network of young professionals in the capital. The audience was young, and consistent with the semi-democratic essence of the confederation, both of the Facebook opponents on the podium were really semi-pro. The moderator opened with the question of how many in the audience already had a Facebook account. Practically all hands went up. The guy next to me made it look like he momentarily wanted to scratch the back of his head. I winced. What, et tu, Brute, even you're on Facebook? Staszek did have some excuses ready.

The male Facebook opponent on the podium, a casually dressed Miguel, read in incomprehensible English from the articles of the American company. The female opponent, a fussy one, admitted that she herself was on Facebook, but rather supported teenager safety regulations.

Both of the Facebook supporters, romantically called "tree huggers", complied with all of my wildest fantasies. "They are completely plasticised", I jostled Staszek. "Look for yourself, they don't even have pores!" Staszek agreed. His sad shake of the head, normally soft and slow, was more intense this time. The two Facebook advocates on the podium looked like business-twins with fancy glasses and blue ties; thin and smooth, without facial expressions.

They were as pleasant as pharmaceutical sales reps from Mars, however rhetorically they were superior. They frequently used the word "modern". "The future brings even more technology, if we take human nature into consideration", they said. They praised different Facebook tools: "If you don't want someone, you can easily remove them. You decide."

Towards the end, we voted, the tree huggers won with twenty-four against twelve. The moderator ended with the words: "Exchange Facebook profiles if you want!" There was a simple buffet; people were dunking crisps into dip. With slight reluctance, I closed in on the tree huggers. I asked them if they had any connection with Scientology. "What makes you think that?" they asked me back. "Well, they're also modern, technology savvy and dynamic." – "That's a good one", I got as a reply. They said that they had nothing at all to do with Scientology.

I wished to scold Facebook even further. I wanted to mention the female Hungarian intern, twenty-two, two hundred "friends". After the podium discussion, we took Zsófia to "Eurotrash", a party brand of the young European people of Brussels, also originating in Facebook. Staszek still had his car back then, and still no woman. He told me at the Eurotrash-party that he found the young Hungarian with the red shoes attractive. Selflessly, I suggested to him that I would excuse myself, go to the toilets, but then not come back for a while and instead linger by the drunken karaoke of some boot-wearing English women. That's how it went down. Somehow he must have done something wrong though. When I saw her later on, Zsófia accused me: "How could you leave me alone with your friend for so long! He kept on talking about Polish-Hungarian friendships the whole time!"

The next time I saw Zsófia, I mocked Facebook again. I said that Facebook devalues the concept of friendship, collecting friends is an infantile regression back to the sandbox principle of: "Would you like to be my friend?" – "You are my friend." – "You are not my friend." The Hungarian intern supported me completely. And spent the following day on Facebook. I could go on scolding as much as I wanted.

Now, however, my English translator was dead at the age of fifty-five. His translations were better than my originals, he was to translate my columns from Brussels. At three am, I read in his in memoriam, he left a description on Facebook of a life-stoned happiness that had come over him under a full moon in a Viennese alley. Three days later, he was dead. If it hadn't been for Facebook, I wouldn't have known that he was happy again before his death. But still, something out there scares me.

The Fire

In May 2009, I was evacuated from the headquarters of the European Commission together with three thousand people. The Berlaymont fire didn't take any casualties, so I am not reporting on a great adventure. The only thing great is the institution in question.

The European Commission bears the appropriate title "sui generis". Never before in history had an establishment been "one of a kind", a supranational government agency with its own excellencies, right of initiative and a corps of civil servants hired for life. Ministers and delegates come and go, but the Commission officials stay. Even though they're only small cogs in a big wheel, the elections can't harm them. The civil servants of the European Commission stand for stability in the comings and goings of the European bubble.

It's too little known that the Commission can actually make us immortal, through "Adonis". Adonis, not meaning the divinely beautiful youth, nor the "Accurate Diagnosis of prostate cancer using Optoacoustic detection of biologically functionalized gold Nanoparticles". Adonis is an archive in the European Commission. To those who don't want to be forgotten after departing this world, write a letter to the European Commission.

Regardless of what the letter contains, the communication department DG COMM will save it for one hundred and twenty plus eight years. The one hundred and twenty years constitute the maximum life span of a European. The eight years are a necessary buffer, since the Commission agenda should be life prolonging. Today people don't have to create a piece of art or commit genocide in order to come closer to immortality. One correctly sent letter to the European Commission is enough. In any case, even without correspondence, the Commission officials look after us with a steady hand. But now: what do they do when the cabin is on fire?

On this very Monday I was at "minus 1", the windowless basement press centre rooms. The Commission spokesmen's "Midday Briefing" was already over. Even this event, called "the midday mass" by veterans, is "sui generis". Supposedly you can't find this anywhere else: a government agency informing the public about their work on a daily basis.

I was sitting in the Wi-Fi room. It began to smell like smoke, like burning plastic. A couple of journalists went to check it out, couldn't find anything and went back to work. Everything seemed normal, there was no alarm going off. I realised that I had heard something shortly before. An object had fallen to the floor; simultaneously someone had shouted something. I noticed that since I had never heard anyone shout in the Berlaymont before. This house is devoid of emotions.

We kept typing away on our laptops. The burnt smell started to become unpleasant. At one point, the bearded warrior of the journalists' union plucked up the courage to call on us to leave, "otherwise we'll get poisoned". When I arrived at the lobby, the evacuation of the three thousand people was almost complete. The security service forced me to the front of the building, from there to the other side of the street. Black smoke was rising from the Berlaymont's roof.

The evacuated civil servants were all quite calm, many were grinning. The evacuation had hit them in the middle of the lunch break, at one o'clock. One said that the fire had started on the thirteenth floor, the President of the Commission's floor. I joined the cafeteria cooks. I had always wanted to get to know them; they represented another of the Commission's peculiarities. Even though the government agency was drawing up regulations against discrimination with constant diligence, you couldn't find the dozens of millions dark-skinned Europeans anywhere in their alignments. The officialdom of the EU is a white man's fort. This was only different amongst the female cooks from the external company "Eurest". At least one of them was black, some spoke Arabic.

We were forced to a park, the cooking ladies and I. The ladies said that they knew where the fire had broken out.

"Oh yeah? Where?" – "In Barroso's kitchen." They sounded convincing. The image of the small Commission's President with the trusting eyes, cracking two eggs in a pan and accidentally setting the shack on fire, created a cheerful atmosphere.

Later that day there was to be a press conference in the glass palace Charlemagne about the fire. No one could really grasp the firemen's explanation of the fire breaking out in the basement but then flaring up on the roof. The alarm had initially gone off on the President of the Commission's floor, and Barroso had been evacuated. Barroso's spokesperson, a super-brain with a minuscule nose and a giant forehead, dealt with the press conference with his hairs on end. Then came my thirty seconds of fame; I confronted Barroso's spokesperson with my exclusive piece of inside information. The idiots from the European press broke out into laughter. The spokesperson retorted: "There is no such thing as 'Barroso's kitchen.'" The President of the Commission doesn't have a kitchen, merely a "hospitality room".

The afternoon before this press conference was long. I had coffee with a Commission acquaintance; he didn't normally have that much time. Afterwards, I had lunch in a popular local pub, which sold veggie dominated organic dishes wrapped in plastic. On the pavement in front of the pub were tables and chairs. I sat down to eat; the smoke from the burning Berlaymont reached my nostrils. No one was agitated.

An elderly gentleman addressed me from the next table. He combined much of what was overrepresented in the

Valley of the Eurocrats: he was environmental lobbyist, homosexual and hated Brussels. He was very friendly towards me. He could guess my age with alarming exactness, up to one and a half months. He wasn't at all interested in the fire. He gave me his number. He complimented me on my looks. He stroked my forearm. The calm hand of the European Commission, this Monday I experienced it.

Why Sliven?

Under the embankment of the Brussels-North railway station, a seedy street is winding, called rue d'Aerschot. "This is no urinal", is written in pink here and there. Almost all houses have shop windows, in which prostitutes are sitting.

Small packs of young men roam the street. They're calling out obscene requests to the windowpanes, deriding the girls with looks and gestures, venting their spleens. The prostitutes smile. They are Europeans.

Rue d'Aerschot only makes out a fraction of prostitution in Brussels. Some two hundred women are working behind the windows. About seventy percent of them are Bulgarians, and further seventy percent of those are from one single eastern Bulgarian city. Altogether, two thousand prostitutes are identified to be from Sliven in the greater Brussels area. A study by the Bulgarian "Center for the Study of Democracy" estimates the number of Sliven prostitutes working abroad to about one thousand. This means that every fifteenth or every seventh woman from

Sliven within a certain age group is prostituting herself. I could not get these numbers out of my head.

But why are there so many prostitutes from Sliven, I asked at the local police station. The Schaerbeek police confirmed the numbers to me. The pimps are from Sliven as well. But why from Sliven, I persisted. "It was a poor village", the policeman replied, "which has become rich this way." Sliven, "the city of wind and gypsies", is however not a village. It has one hundred thousand inhabitants.

Poverty and unemployment, that was the first explanation, I was to hear it more often. It never satisfied me. There are poor people elsewhere too, yet Polish women come to Brussels to clean and Polish men don't become pimps, but plumbers. The explanation was also bad since some women who could be seen sitting in the windows of the European capital were university alumni and graduates from the Sliven Foreign Languages Secondary School. The latter is an elite school. With such a diploma, there are other jobs to be found.

Why Sliven, I asked at Bulgaria's representation to the EU. The spokeswoman called me up, her voice quivered with outrage. "Do you *really* want to portray Bulgaria through *prostitutes*?" she shouted into the phone. I had involuntarily offended a lady. In the beginning of 2009, the Bulgarian government agency had already been offended by the piece of art "Entropa", of the Czech Council presidency. The Turkish toilet representing Bulgaria therefore had to be covered with a black cloth. I apologised. I brought to her attention that it could be important to the Bulgarian image in Europe, if ten thousand citizens and visitors of Brussels get to know the Balkan nation exclusively through sex for money. I got no reply. Other Bulgarian agencies kept quiet as well. I was never to get an answer from official Bulgaria again.

I wandered a couple of times around the Brussels-North station. In the steep alleys around rue de la Prairie sat the black prostitutes. Along the railway embankment, in rue d'Aerschot, sat the Europeans. Only a couple, maybe even none, looked like they were Roma. The prostitutes were sitting in the windows, on barstools mostly. They smiled sweetly, one was luring with obscene tongue gestures, some tapped invitingly on their side of the glass. A couple were ravishingly beautiful, others really looked like elite school graduates.

In order to get a better understanding, I went there with Liliana and Staszek. The bored Romanian, promising candidate for a steady position in the Commission, found this interesting. She translated the indignities to me, which the Romanian onlookers were shouting at the windows. Staszek did me a great favour by coming along. He still didn't have a girlfriend, yet he pursued dating Flemish and English women. I couldn't have done him any worse than dragging him down this street. Deeply depressed, he followed me, with his shoulders slack. He helped me though, spoke to people for me, assisted in the research with his hundred languages.

I spoke to the punters. The majority were young foreigners, walking and driving through in groups. They had never heard of Sliven. I had them explain the procedure to me. It lasts fifteen minutes. It takes place behind a curtain, the costumer can hear the other women chattering and moaning. The price is forty euros, for fifty a change of position is included. Blowjob with rubber, lube, penetration. The women don't let themselves be kissed, anywhere. In order for the costumer to ejaculate quickly, they automatically begin to moan. In the showroom, always decorated as a comfortable living room, an idle colleague is tattling in the meantime with a respectable gammer sitting around there. The role of these old ladies isn't clear right away. When the fifteen minutes are up, an alarm goes off. At the end the woman asks the costumer: "ça va, chéri?"

I spoke to one prostitute from Sliven, young, beautiful, dark curls. "Why are there so many from Sliven working here?" I asked. She had by no means studied at the Foreign Languages Secondary School, she explained, she only visited Sliven for her holidays. Why Sliven, I asked again. How can one single city provide a notable part of the Netherlands and the metropolis Brussels with prostitutes? "C'est comme ça", she retorted, "that's how it is." That answer didn't satisfy me. I decided I would travel to Sliven that summer.

In the Container

In order to get the following story, I passed myself off as a banker. That was a lie; I'm anything but a banker. There just wasn't any other way.

Rome, Byzantium, Moscow, Brussels – on the one hand this line-up makes sense. On the other hand, the fourth capital is missing the emotion-inspiring gesture of imperial politics. The Eurocrats don't declare any wars or make stadiums roar with their speeches. They don't have gladiators, nor court ceremony, their harmless approaches to show trials still don't look very impressive. Then for once they have this world sensation – and they won't let me in.

A crisis was going on outside. The EU governments supported fifty banks with four hundred billion euros and provided guarantee schemes of two thousand three hundred billion. Every single grant had to be approved by the European Commission, by the competition authority DG COMP. They didn't have the resources for this. And now to the sensation: the negotiations took place in an inner courtyard. The boards of directors and bank solicitors were auditioning inside containers.

The people concerned called the containers "torture chambers", wrote the *Financial Times*. Chairs made of hard plastic, Formica tables, plastic mugs. The persons summoned had to sit there for many long hours. There was nothing to eat, the bankers complained, not even cookies. I didn't rest until I could see the inside of the containers.

I lurked about rue Joseph II. At number 27 the usual: DG EMPL, colourful display boards about "gender", "inclusion", "fighting discrimination". It is completely different at number 70, a green and chic building, shimmering as if plasticised. The DG COMP didn't need any self-promotion, after fines of billions of euros for Microsoft and Intel, the competition authority conveyed respect. In the tortured dunning ensemble of governesses that is the European Commission, the DG COMP played the part of the cool bitch.

I peeked through the high black metal fence of the gateway into the inner courtyard. I saw six blue office containers, lined up seamlessly, behind them some more. At four o'clock, business was still going. Occasionally someone came out, inconspicuous people between the ages of thirty and forty. Most of the windows were shaded. I could make out a PowerPoint presentation. Toxic papers? I stared through the fence. No trifles were being negotiated inside the containers, I had learned from the *Financial Times*, the DG COMP wanted to coerce some banks to boil down the balance sheet total to half. I came back a couple of times. I pleaded with the spokesperson to let me in. Not a chance.

I turned to the company that constructed the containers, "de Meeuw" – "the seagull". They didn't respond so I just went there. It took me three hours to go thirty kilometres. Two different regional trains, at the final destination Willebroek train station, only a taxi was of further use. I didn't like going to Flanders, I didn't affiliate anything good with that place.

In winter I had lived for some time at a Flemish girl's house, my tenth bedstead, in a calm bourgeois part of Ixelles. She was a solicitor at a big law firm and a distant acquaintance of the French-speaking Alessia. The Walloon-Flemish contrast couldn't be illustrated any louder than through the alleged friends. The solicitor didn't treat me badly; I got her vacant "Teenage Room" at a fair price. She was just slightly organically obsessed and had a hard to grasp regiment of plastic bags and plastic cups in different colours. What bothered me was how she would talk about the smallest and the largest things in life in an exactly identical manner. Whether she was talking about falling in love or about getting reimbursed on her electrical bill thanks to frugal energy usage, she would speak with the same amount of excitement.

Other than that not many good things come to mind about Flanders in general. On the whole I'm a bad European, unlike the Eurocrats with their imperturbable balance, I either love the sound of a language or hate it. Regarding the sound of Flemish, no means of escape seemed too farfetched. Whenever I stopped in a Flemish town, I was agonising for a word to describe what I saw. There's the word despair, there's the word depression, but to describe the faces of the passers-by in Flemish cities, as of yet language doesn't have a word.

I really didn't like to go to Flanders. I had to wait for the taxi in the town Willebroek. First, I saw a big election sign of Vlaams Belang; a grateful looking child with rosy cheeks painted with the Flemish colours. Alongside it read: "Dit is ons land." No problem, I thought to myself, I definitely won't take it away from you. I wanted to kill time over a cup of coffee. The only pub close to the station was called "Shanghai", the Chinese host refused to let me in. I couldn't get any coffee, he explained harshly, "ici restaurant".

The city, which I then rushed through by cab, was composed of small red brick houses and straight levelled streets. The streets reminded me of a Lilliput railway. I landed directly on the blocked highway between Antwerp and Brussels. Five minutes before closing time, I arrived.

The assistant sales manager was called out. I explained to him that I was the Brussels Public Affairs spearhead of a major bank and that the bank was considering the container solution after having experienced the courtyard example. He smiled proudly. The moment after, I was in. I stood inside the unit the DG COMP used, the "Flexicom". The Commission had chosen the middle class unit. Plenty of outlets, one white light tube and a white radiator, all included. Minimum rental was four weeks, after three to four years it was cheaper to buy. One alternative even came with a Port-a-Loo.

The young man said that people had false impressions of containers. The Seagull builds everything out of containers, for example schools, and the hospital St. Niklaas as well. They were currently building a new head office with several floors out of the premium unit "K21". In passing, the sales assistant showed me a dingy box, half taken apart, barely heatable, with an outer wall made out of dirty fine rib. "We don't sell those anymore", he explained, "we send them to Romania."

The company was closing. I went down to the Flemish highway and waited for a taxi. I was satisfied. Rome, Byzantium, Moscow, container – such thrilling times, we are so lucky!

The Beds

While there was an election campaign for the European Parliament going on out in the Member States, an offer reached me inside the capital: I was to stay in the Brusselian flat of an MEP, a Member of the European Parliament.

The offer came from the acquaintance of a distant acquaintance. I didn't know the representative; he was on election tour in his home country. I also didn't know his country very well. I immediately accepted and rejoiced, I would launch into the European election campaign of Brussels from the very home of a genuine Member of the European Parliament.

I had after all been moving around the city like a nomad the whole year. Never did I have anything more than one suitcase with me. That was intentional; I wanted to figure out the Eurocrats and lobbyists by also observing their private way of living. Would I otherwise know how long they showered?

The nomad lifestyle went well for a long time. I always had a roof over my head. Sure, there were places that I more than gladly left after a couple of nights. If I were vicious, I would describe the attempt to a walk through Woluwe-Saint Lambert, a popular residential area for Eurocrats. The streets were named after months. On every corner there was a small petrol station with room for two and a half compact cars, the streets were quiet like a graveyard, and if I ran into someone it was Monsieur Jean-Marie, a petty bourgeois Belgian with his small neurotic dog.

I also stayed in the house of a Commission official, near the institutions. Imagine him as a good-looking man in his mid-thirties, popular with the ladies. He had had his piece of real estate elaborately reconstructed. When I got to know him he fascinated me with the assertion that his house was so narrow, that when he stretched out his arms he could reach both walls with his fingertips.

That was conceivable in Brussels. He had made that up though, in truth his house was 3.2 metres wide. The staircase indeed took up a quarter of the space; he spent a significant portion of his life on the stairs. The house looked two storeys high from the outside, but in fact on the inside, the civil servant had five floors all to himself. The second and the third floor were wrested from the first floor and floors four and five from the second. You could stand for ages in this house and look and wonder about its construction. Before shaking anyone's hand, the civil servant washed his own. Consequently, there were showers installed on floors one, three and five, and there were different kinds of sanitary facilities on every floor.

The nomad lifestyle went genuinely well for a long time. The more people I knew, the more options I had. Once, I withdrew to a former monastery for a couple of days. The monastery had since become a hostel for foreigners, who liked the strict leadership of a puritanical white-haired American woman. It was Staszek who made me aware of this adults' orphanage's existence. The unhappy guy had just moved there, he had become a "resident" of the "ICA".

We were all shocked that Staszek suddenly didn't come to the six-thirty-receptions anymore, since Mother Superior summoned for supper at seven o'clock. Staszek explained that he wanted to get rid of some dead weight, that he wanted to be free for a post-Brussels era. He constantly thought about quitting his post in the EU. He gathered all his remaining holidays and flew restlessly through Europe. Everywhere he liked it better, everywhere he wanted to live. After his holidays in Turkey, he surprised me by having small talk in Turkish in a Brusselian night shop. After a flight to Moscow he imagined Russian pillow talk, his Russian abilities did no longer stand in his way. In the meantime he stayed in Brussels and suffered.

I got a cell in the "Bed & Breakfast" wing. The cell was expensive, the wing stood empty. When resident Staszek saw my cell he turned pale with envy. I had a reading light, such luxury the residents had to procure for themselves. Upon my arrival, Mother Superior had informed me that smoking was only allowed in the garden. When I left three days later, the regime had already turned less liberal. Smoking in the garden was then only allowed standing up, next to two designated ashtrays attached to the monastery wall.

The nomad lifestyle went genuinely well for a really long time. I got carefree and rarely planned ahead. In the merry month of May, I was suddenly out on the street. It was Monday, the hotels in this mother of all conference cities were expensive. It was night. I didn't know where to go.

The only thing that came to mind was the poster of a hotel by the hour, which I had noticed in the streetwalker district, Alhambra. Twenty euros for three hours; thirty-five euros for the whole night. If that was correct, it was an unrivalled price. Staszek let me leave my suitcase with him at the monastery. Then I went to Alhambra. I rang the doorbell.

Alhambra, "5th Avenue", would be my nineteenth sleeping place in Brussels. I felt stupid, with a laptop and no woman, but they took me in indifferently. The house was a wonder made of red velvet tapestry. Soft old Russian pop sounded through the building. I asked about that. They found the music erotic, but didn't know any Russian.

I went up the narrow creaking stairs to my room. I didn't hear any moaning. A male Arabic voice was insulting an almost inaudible woman. In my room, I discovered a four-poster bed facing a big mirror. The beige and flower-decorated chairs were fit for kings. Behind a red drapery I found a basin and a boudoir. A diffused picture hung on the wall, portraying a seemingly French blonde, squatting naked, covering herself with a skin-coloured nothing of a shawl. I lay down on the bed and observed myself in the mirror. What a revival after always wandering through the sterilised Valley of the Eurocrats! Here should a European Carrie Bradshaw put up, I thought, here the columnist would get going for real. Get going with the real stories from the meat market in the Eurocrat valley; get going with "Sex and the Valley". I slept like a baby.

The hotel by the hour was not a long-term solution. I was therefore happy to step into my twentieth lodging, near the church Saint-Antoine, in an ethnically mixed corner of Etterbeek. I found the key in the mailbox. I saw the name of the absent delegate for the first time then. I was very pleased with myself. It seemed quite extraordinary to me to go into the Europe campaign of Brussels from the flat of an unknown Member of the European Parliament.

The first impression was pleasant. The biggest room, which served as bedroom, faced a green and contorted terrace-balcony tree-world. Shortly after I was startled, because that was it. Three doors led to a tiny toilet, a tiny bathroom, a tiny kitchen. The shower curtain was wildly hung over the boiler's outlet pipe. The kitchen's existence I completely blocked out of my head after the first look, it was minuscule and dingy and smelled like fumes from the seventies.

I had pictured the domicile of a member of the second largest democratically elected parliament in the world differently. I saw banners and stickers from his country, the storage table looked like an altar covered by the blue flag of the confederation. Over the king size bed hung a world map according to the Human Development Index.

Furthermore photos of ducks in a lake, printed sayings by Voltaire, Einstein and *Yahoo's* CEO. The man seemed to be young.

I started to look at the neighbourhood through the eyes of my affiliated MEP. An Arabian mother was yelling in a bloodcurdling manner from a balcony higher up, she was actually just on the phone. Construction workers joked around in Romanian. Did the delegate possibly know of the clamorous cluster of Internet cafés next door? He had no laundry machine, no TV, no Internet at the house, I therefore frequently visited these shops. Once, an African woman was cowering under the counter in one of the cafés, her face averted, strangely sobbing. The Arabic owner explained to me with helpless emotion: "She just learned that her baby died in Africa."

Through the eyes of the delegate, I went down to the European Parliament, through rue de l'Orient or Morgenlandstraat, by the immigrant's vegetable shops, towards this silver-shimmering colossus, to the probably largest building in Europe. Did my parliamentarian look back on this sixth period of Parliament with pride? On the Chemical Regulation "Reach", on the visit of the Dalai Lama, on the climate change package? On the "initiative report" of the prohibition of housewives in advertising? On a period, which began with the prevention of Catholic Commissioner Buttiglione and ended with the just-failed conviction of the Pope?

On top of a knick-knack cupboard belonging to my delegate I saw a large Virgin Mary and an icon. Suddenly, I wanted to know where the man stood ideologically, who hung posters of a "condom safari" in his vestibule. I looked through voting lists. I couldn't find him anywhere. I met up with the distant acquaintance. Oh, what wails, my MEP never was one! He worked in the apparatus of the Parliament and was only running for a position in the European Parliament. His candidature was not even promising. All I had assumed up until that point was wrong.

I turned towards the election campaign in Brussels. Portraits of candidates were hanging in the shop windows. No slogans were written underneath, only the names and numbers of the candidates. Half of the Brusselians were born outside of Belgium – that came through in all of its colourful diversity. Even the Christian Democrats, since then relabelled "Humanists", promoted themselves with Fatimas and Amals, with Mutyebeles and Lumbalas.

I steered towards the Arabic neighbourhood of Anderlecht, to an election meeting of the leading party in Brussels, the Socialists. *Le Soir* published up-to-date sociodemographic maps. It was easy to confuse the two maps; unemployment rate of forty percent and Moroccan neighbourhoods were both coloured in dark red.

Amongst others, Fallida was sitting on the podium, a Minister of Culture; of which there are a total of three in Brussels. The new working class, elderly Moroccan gentlemen, were listening to the young denim-wearing Moroccan woman with expectant faces. I found out that Brussels is rich, and its citizens unemployed; commuters from Flanders and Wallonia occupied more than half of the Brusselian workplaces. Almost all politicians in Brussels proposed a taxation of the commuters for the city's salvation.

I didn't hear anything about Europe; the Brusselian election campaign was focused on the simultaneously scheduled regional elections. Regarding the European elections, I could only account for their absence. You can hate Brussels for this, but maybe you should love the capital even more: the plasticisers will find it a hard nut to crack.

The Hans-Gert-Machine

On the evening of 7 June 2009, I went to the European Parliament. It was election night, I expected a party. The Parliament is young, female, attractive, all other institutions pale in comparison. It is rumoured of the Italian delegates in particular that they prefer dividing their assistant positions into four parts with eight long legs. Add to that the female interns, together with the male interns numbering two thousand five hundred per year. One of them shared a shocking secret with me.

The party itself was devastatingly tepid. Not even Hans-Gert was there. Hans-Gert Pöttering, the assigned President of Parliament, born in 1945, a divorced Catholic from Osnabruck, in the European Parliament since 1979, the only one who has been present since the beginning of direct elections. I don't know him personally but call him by his first name, since nothing could describe him better than the hyphen between Hans and Gert. It has been written about him that he could talk a room into a coma within ten minutes. That was mean. He might not have stood out with positions. After 7 June 2009, I knew: there was more to Hans-Gert.

So; the party. Nothing was served in the crowded corridors. Videos were being played for the journalists in the plenary room, Hans-Gert at the elections. The television channel, which the Parliament had treated itself, interviewed Belgian ex-premiers and reeled-in schoolgirls.

I saw the old Swede whom I saw everywhere. He wasn't much to look at, a chunky man, constantly with a champagne glass in his hand. Once, he was introduced to me by an acquaintance as the man "who heaves sunken treasures from the bottom of the ocean". Fifteen minutes later, he was introduced to me by another acquaintance as "representative of the Zimbabwean opposition in Brussels". Both times, the Swede had nodded graciously. On the night of the election, he stood with an elegant Ukrainian woman. She said: "I have never experienced such a badly organised election night." He nodded graciously.

Hans-Gert's Conservatives won the European elections, the Socialists were thrashed all across Europe. Once again, people complained about the voter participation. Only one American was wondering how after all forty-three percent elected a Parliament whose semi-legislative functions don't stand in any comprehensible relation to the governance of the EU.

I got to know a female intern. Well hello there, she was a member of Hans-Gert's staff of forty! She had jug ears, the waist of a wasp and an uncle in the city council of

Osnabruck. She had only seen the President of the Parliament twice. Her office was situated well below his glorious seat in the sky.

I got to know the female intern at the Greens' buffet. She was standing there with another intern from a news portal, an arduous shaker of hands, just as omnipresent as the old Swede. The intern reported indignantly how he had been thrown out of the Socialists' buffet, after eight years of party membership. He hadn't brought his membership-book with him; however, he wanted to switch to the Greens anyway. He shared my assessment that the European Parliament was a paradise for the Greens.

And suddenly, the revelation. The female intern told me that she had already written several interviews for Hans-Gert. "Yes, me too", the other intern joined in, "I wrote the speech for the fifty-year celebration of the German Technical Inspection Association for him." It's very easy, the two interns explained, both of which voted for the Greens. You just take an old Hans-Gert interview, which was perhaps already written by a member of the Green movement, and construct it into something new. I felt weak at the knees. I remembered how much by Hans-Gert I had skimmed through, in the most remote printed matters in Europe. Hans-Gert was more than a human, I understood. Everyone around me was Hans-Gert.

The female intern took me to the Conservatives' drinks. Only cherry beer was left. The intern had one cherry beer after the other, but not even then could she think of any dirty office stories. Hans-Gert left after the election. Some Jerzy person was elected in his place, and for a few days, Staszek looked at the future of Europe with pride and confidence. Those are details though. The Hans-Gert-machine keeps on running.

That's Why Sliven

Under the embankment of the Brussels-North railway station, a seedy street is winding, called rue d'Aerschot. Almost all houses have shop windows, and two hundred prostitutes are sitting in them. Seventy percent of them come from one single Bulgarian city, Sliven. No one in Brussels could tell me why that many women from Sliven prostituted themselves. The question wouldn't leave me alone. So, in July 2009 I set out. I went to Sliven.

I came from the coast through a barren, not too intensely cultivated plain almost completely devoid of trees. When I saw the ruggedly towering cliffs of the "Blue Rocks", I had reached my goal. It was hot. The northern winds from several Balkan passes all come together in Sliven, however on those summer days nothing was refreshing, at best the shade from the mature trees along the trimmed boulevard. Sliven wasn't ugly. The spacious fauteuil-landscape of the restaurants induced relaxation. Poverty and unemployment, the explanation for the extensive Sliven prostitution given to me by the Brusselian police, seemed less convincing than ever before. The view I had of the young women from Sliven was intolerable to me. Many were dressed provocatively, just like elsewhere. I couldn't get the question out of my head whether I was looking at former or soon-to-be whores on holidays.

In the beginning, the writer Janina Dragostinova from Sofia helped me find my way through the city. It was the weekend of a Bulgarian Parliament election. Once again, the Bulgarians succumbed to a saviour, this time to the former bodyguard of the Communist dictator Todor Zhivkov. The man who had managed to get forty percent straightaway was massive and shaved. He spoke slowly and to the point and could barely walk for all his strength. I constantly heard "Bruksel", Brussels, being mentioned on TV. This Bruksel had frozen certain aid for Bulgaria, because of corruption. The bodyguard had named his party "Citizens for European Development of Bulgaria". He promised to clean up and re-establish the cash flow from Brussels.

An editor in chief from Sofia on election tour gave me the most farfetched answer. The Sliven area is a centre for the Karakachans, who the local Bulgarians had introduced to labour migration. The Karakachans are shepherds, speaking an archaic form of Greek. "They are so pious, that they've worn black ever since the Byzantine Empire was occupied by infidels." They would never be accused of pimping though.

We went to a nearby village. Dragodanovo was flat, poor, drab. A few expensive cars, but there was nothing confirming Dragodanovo's reputation – that literally every good-looking girl was going to be a prostitute abroad.

The villagers I spoke to acted oblivious. In the village café booze heads were sitting, babbling nonsense. They gave me answer number three: "That's democracy." Democracy – what they really meant was capitalism – was responsible for prostitution. But why Dragodanovo, why Sliven, isn't there democracy elsewhere as well? I wanted to leave but Janina signalled me over to another table. She had made a man talk. He was younger, smarter and dressed neater. Years ago, he used to be an errand boy for the most famous Sliven pimp in Brussels. This Atanas Mundev had survived eight bullets and was placed under house arrest at the time of my visit.

The former errand boy told me that the profit from the prostitution was invested in drugs, Dutch ecstasy for Bulgaria, Turkish heroin for the West. He too spoke of democracy and cited figures that the women from the Sliven area supposedly earned, unrealistically high figures. He said that, the "white men in Brussels" lusted for the exotic features of a darker woman, that's why the prostitutes would tan themselves. I uttered quiet doubts, regarding the "white men in Brussels"; many of the sex buyers are Arabs. I could confirm that most of the prostitutes in rue d'Aerschot were very tanned. At home, they stick to this habit, said the errand boy. "The tanning salons in Sliven were all opened by former prostitutes."

Back in Sliven I was introduced to someone whose identity I swore to protect. I will only call her "the source". The source had experienced the brutal onsets in the nineties. Back then, fat old sex tourists from Italy and Germany had been brought minors in "Chateau Alpia", Todor Zhivkov's former Sliven residence. She had protected a fugitive girl, the source told me, whereupon someone had thrown a rock at her head in the park. The source gave me answer number four: "There's a gym in Sliven which produced internationally successful boxers. After the reunification, the guys lost their social status. They didn't know what to do with their strength. They turned to other things, racketeering and pimping."

Meanwhile, the power balance has shifted since the pimps didn't dare use force anymore. "Now it's the girls who go looking for a pimp, not the other way around." The source solved the riddle of the respectable grandmas sitting behind the Brusselian shop windows: "They are retired accountants and school teachers. They collect the money for the pimps." These grandmas were called "Madamkas".

On the Sunday of the election, I stumbled into an obscure game. A freckly beanpole, municipal representative for the right-extremist protest party "Ataka", introduced himself with the words: "I don't exist." He asked me into his rickety Lada and drove me up the mountain. He stopped in front of a mountain lodge. It was a vertical little castle made out of chilling raw stone. It was "Chateau Alpia", Todor Zhivkov's former residence.

A gentleman joined us, the same type of man as the bodyguard saviour shortly before elected Prime Minister. The gentleman introduced himself as a businessman, a greengrocer. He said there were three hundred pimps in Sliven. His sister-in-law reported one of them in the Netherlands, he had then thrown a bomb into the greengrocer's garden.

He remained vague regarding the subject of his sister-in-law's prostitution. "The pimp hadn't paid her anything." – "Nothing at all?" – "Well, fine, he had paid her a little." The greengrocer didn't want to introduce me to his sister-in-law; he had a different request. I was to name all the Sliven police men, who he accused of corruption, in the newspapers. I couldn't promise him that. He didn't seem very trustworthy to me.

To my recurrent question – why so many from Sliven? – I got a couple more explanations. The fifth answer, "they're gypsies", came from the patriotic schoolteacher of an "elite technical school". Indeed there was a Roma neighbourhood in Sliven, indeed many a young Rom waxed lyrically about there being "no sweeter money" than pimping, yet this answer was wrong. The study by "Center for the Study of Democracy" maintained that a minority of the prostitutes from Sliven were Roma. I told the teacher that the skin colours in rue d'Aerschot were reversed. The punters rather Oriental, the prostitutes rather white. Annoyed, she pulled a face.

I found a graduate from the elitist Foreign Languages Secondary School. She said that she didn't know any prostitutes in her class. What the student told me might have been an approximation though, an approximation of a possible change of values of a Sliven kind: "Many of my fellow students are very good-looking. They have significantly older boyfriends, often restaurant owners. Two classmates have gotten breast implants as presents. No one asked the parents."

After all these conversations, what was missing was the most obvious of all; a prostitute from Sliven. I met with a local reporter, who gave me the seventh answer. The reporter pronounced my numbers as "nonsense" and the topic as "exhausted". He claimed that by no means did above-average numbers of prostitutes come from Sliven. He didn't know any and also didn't know where to find them. He added: "I trust the police."

After Janina Dragostinova had left, I was on my own. The stream of stories ebbed out; I began to have doubts. On several occasions, I wandered through "Little Amsterdam", a residential street near the city centre, allegedly the preferred retreat for former prostitutes. There were many shops with children's fashion and several tanning salons in the freshly painted pastel-coloured blocks of flats. I stepped into the tanning salons and asked: "Parlez-vous français?" No one affirmed. Only the plastic flower arrangements, which they had put on display, reminded me of the Brusselian shop windows in rue d'Aerschot.

Even though I was less trusting than the local reporter, I still went to the Sliven police. The greengrocer was a previously convicted pimp, the officers told me, the bomb in his garden had been a firecracker. I spoke to one of the officers specialised in trafficking. He estimated the number of women from Sliven in rue d'Aerschot to be somewhat lower, but confirmed most of the facts. The disappearance of forced prostitution, the phenomenon "Foreign Languages Secondary School", the phenomenon "Madamka". He said that the establishments themselves were mostly owned by Russians. A prostitute earned "no more than seven thousand euros per month". The money was brought to Bulgaria by cash couriers in coaches and then invested in real estate.

The man sounded rational, I involuntarily started to trust him. He said that he had heard two schoolgirls talking on the street. "One said to the other: when I'm eighteen, I'll go to Brussels, and then I'll have a cool car too." He thus introduced the eighth answer. By now, there are young couples from Sliven who go to Brussels for some months to walk the streets freelance. "Why do they do that?" I asked. The police officer hesitated. "They probably think it's modern. They want to experiment with themselves."

Nothing seemed more impossible than finding a prostitute in Sliven. The last night of my stay, I found out for myself what Sliven had to offer in terms of prostitution. It was a streetwalkers' patch with just three women, broken Roma from the twenty-thousand inhabitant slum "Hope".

I went with one of them. She had never heard of Bruksel. She said that she was twenty, but looked like forty. She said that she was currently nursing her second child. In a park nearby, her pimp emerged from the shadows. It was her brother. I would have liked to be spared the later course of the evening. When I confessed to the woman that I didn't want any sex, the situation turned into begging, long and painful.

The road to bed however brought me a ninth answer, my own. For quite some time, the little pimp couldn't find the flat where he was taking his sister and me. Eventually, we were standing in a dark stairway of a bourgeois house, eventually a door opened.

A respectable grandmother in a nightgown greeted us, with freshly plucked eyebrows. She was extremely friendly, charged two euros fifty for rent and showed us to the made-up bed. It crossed my mind that this grandma looked exactly like the Brusselian "Madamkas". Like the neat retirees who are sitting, knitting and chatting behind the windowpanes in rue d'Aerschot. Why so many women from Sliven become prostitutes? I still don't know. If anyone knows, it's the grandmas from Sliven.

The Ditches

I admit that my informant didn't seem all too trustworthy. Vladimir Pasutin was an eastern European businessman. He had made money in agriculture in the Republic of Transnistria, which is internationally considered an illegal secession of Moldavia. He had several bodyguards. He drove a fuel-guzzling car. He wore shades.

I was a guest in his Transnistrian villa. Pasutin suffered from leg complaints, the bodyguard therefore had to haul him out of the four-wheel drive. Pasutin also suffered from claustrophobia, we therefore had to cross a wide living area. First, a pool, then a fantastically big double bed. The fifty-year old was awaited by his young, beautiful, blond wife.

I furthermore admit that Vladimir Pasutin incidentally was a representative in the Parliament of his poorly regarded republic. He liked China, and in order to influence a referendum, he had once hired a group of young demonstrating women. No, you probably wouldn't buy a used car from my informant. But he showed me something. Something nobody else in Europe knows.

It was before I came to Brussels. Pasutin took me through his Transnistrian cornfields. Flat fields, they went on forever. He stopped by a sign in the cornfield: it announced the Ukrainian border. "The EU is indeed fighting smuggle trade between Transnistria and the Ukraine", Pasutin explained. "The EU has therefore ordered a canal from the Ukrainians. Over two hundred kilometres, all along the border."

We stepped out and he showed me a freshly excavated ditch, which ran through the cornfield in a single line. The ditch was barely one metre deep and barely half a metre wide. I didn't have to jump; I could just step over it. Anyone in good health between the ages of seven and seventy-seven could step over it. "That's the canal that the Ukrainians delivered", Pasutin said. "Cost a couple of million for the EU, in return the Ukrainians now have nice cars." He doubled over from laughter.

When I arrived in Brussels, I followed the trace of the ditch. Benita Ferrero-Waldner was the person responsible in the European Commission. Like me, she was from Austria, I did by no means want to find fault with my Commissioner. I just checked with them. I had a picture of the ditch and sent it with my request. In the Commissioner's department, people first had to make enquiries. One week later, the spokeswoman wrote to me that the ditch was financed by the Ukraine. I wanted to meet for an interview with the female expert in charge. Apparently, there was only one expert. After one month I got the meeting.

I stood as agreed in the reception of the glass palace Charlemagne. No one came. Fifteen minutes later the spokeswoman for the Commissioner ran past me. I ran after her. Where had I been, she asked while running, I should have gone upstairs to the expert. Now though, the expert was gone.

I became suspicious. I began to suspect that Pasutin's laughter from hell had involuntarily pushed me into a case of fraud of European dimensions. I already saw myself as an investigating journalist. I enquired at the Transnistrian, the Moldavian, the Ukrainian foreign ministry, at the Ukrainian Presidential department. No answer. I threatened to go to Ukraine's representation to the EU. I was welcome, they told me, but they didn't know anything.

Only EUBAM replied to me, the EU control unit at that border. EUBAM said that they didn't have anything to do with the ditch, I could ask the Ukrainian customs authority. The mail server of the Ukrainian customs authority had crashed and stayed that way for months.

At one point I called the Ukrainian customs authority. I asked them about the ditch. That's no ditch, the spokesperson for the Ukrainian customs authority indignantly replied, that is "an engineered construction". It worked really well; the smugglers couldn't drive over it. They always trench an engineered construction only where smuggling is a current problem. He didn't know anything about the costs. The Ukraine had paid for it.

I admit that I might not have been on to a case of fraud of European dimensions after all. Maybe there isn't that much deception, since everything is evaluated. Pasutin's story was good though. A ditch, which should have become a canal and which now unites more than it separates – that was the better story.

The Murder Ballad of Section Z

There was something else in the capital of the "soft power" EU, in this permanently professional "business-as-usual" administrative centre, in this great faceless cipher. There was something else, with thirty-nine dead: the "Heysel tragedy". Was it an accident? Or was it the Anglo-Italian war of 1985?

I went over there with the Métro, close to the Atomium on the "Discovery trail" of the by now renamed Heysel stadium. A cheerful Belgian with dark skin greeted me. He spoke with pride of how he was trained in the army as an aeroplane technician. He didn't think being a museum attendant in the stadium was that bad either.

He took me through the rooms, set up with little films and sound recordings, which simulated the atmosphere before the game. In the national team's changing room the lockers stood open, the meticulously arranged outfits were fastened. The sign with the name of the national team's coach stood in the press conference room.

"He was discharged", the guide remarked, "the results were too bad."

He took me over to the grandstand. In 1985, the spectators in the Heysel were standing up; now they were sitting on moss-green seats. "We don't have any first-class seats", the guide said, even the King of Belgium has to make do with seats' back rests the height of a hand. The pitch was dirt-brown. The grass was just being rolled out. The Belgian cup finals were coming up. The guide didn't know which teams were playing. Both teams were from Flanders, maybe that was why he wasn't very interested.

He showed me the scene, section Z. "In memoriam 29.05.85" was written on a simple memorial plaque. The wall made of red bricks looked new. Back then it had broken down before the big final game between Liverpool and Juventus. The guide explained: "The English had pushed out of their section, there were too few Belgians in-between." I took note of this. He explicitly blamed the English.

He took me to the "1985 security tower", a couple of metres away. The windowless main room was grey with a green fence. "That's the hooligan prison", my friendly guide said. There was a second cell being built, for female hooligans.

At the end he left me alone in the memorial room. Two artificial wreaths were lying under the plaque, with the names of the dead. Almost all names of the dead on the plaque, thirty-two out of thirty-nine, were Italian.

In the coolness of the memorial room, I exposed myself to the film recordings. As a matter of fact, it was the

English who had let show their ugly side on this bright May day. They went ashore at Ostend, drunk and jeering. A sunburnt and half-naked guy showed his arse to the camera. In the bursting arena, long before kick-off, they started chasing Italians. The Juventus supporters were squeezed together; they were trampled to death.

There were pictures from a dirty, chaotic slaughter. While the dead were being pulled away from section Z, the people still alive were beating on each other on the track and the green. At 7:31 pm, the wall came crashing down, almost three hours later the police officer in charge ordered the kick-off of the game for security reasons.

The Italian footballers refused to play. Eventually they did, true to the slogan: "We will beat the English, after they murdered our fans." Without shoes and covered in blood, one Italian Juventus supporter kept on cheering. Juventus won, Platini converted a penalty kick. English witnesses kept complaining even twenty years later, the penalty had been due to diving by the Italians. After the game, the English supporters were escorted out of Belgium. The Italians stayed in the arena. They celebrated.

After one and a half hours, I stepped out of the memorial room; a bigger part of the Heysel Stadium's grass had been rolled out. The jolly black Belgian said his hearty goodbyes. Football is a beautiful game; it moves almost all people in the world. And still, in May 1985, there was war in Brussels.

The Raid

Originally, I had dreamt of a TV-series: "Sex and the City", with people willing to mate from all over Europe, starring the fairies and brownies of the Eurocrat valley. In Brussels I learned that you have to invent a lot of things, for example sex. Assuming that a TV-station would order the series from me, I would gladly invent sufficiently fantastical things. Though I would be less sure of the title of the series: The Centre? The Lobby? Eurocrats? Place Lux? Eurotrash? Studio Europe? One character was certain however: the coolest guy would be a cartel hunter from the European Commission.

The guys from DG COMP radiate respect. They drew out a car glass manufacturers' cartel, the convicted companies had to pay the record sum of 1.38 billion euros. 1.12 billion euros for the gas cartel. The following businesses were punished for price fixings with fines from 388 up to 855 million: bleach, plasterboards, windowpanes, rubber, paraffin wax, switchgears, vitamins. Through the confiscated money, the Member States' contributions were lowered.

About once a month, the cartel hunters create their most thrilling scene. A "dawn raid" is then carried out, for the most part simultaneously at several places in the European Economic Area. I had both sides describe the procedure to me. It's difficult finding a cartel hunter; as the DG COMP protects their identities. Through semi-private detours I found one who anonymously told me everything on the phone.

He presented himself in an accentuated rational manner. "You find astonishingly little cowboy-mentality amongst us", he said. His colleagues were also "typical civil servants", who "in the end are proud that the consumers are protected". It all depends on the element of surprise. The quick orientation in unknown buildings is crucial, for which they only had *Google maps*. The first minutes are mentally straining. Excited about a raid, the cartel hunter said, is something that he never is.

Luc Rivet, a greying Belgian in a polo shirt, earlier a paper lobbyist in Sweden, since then the general secretary of the lift lobby ELA, was even less excited about it. The big ones in the lift industry had been sentenced to a cartel fine of 992 million. Afterwards, his ELA relocated from the European Quarter to the Brusselian periphery, "where the rents are half the price".

Rivet first of all conveyed the needs of his industry. The man wouldn't be a bad supporting character, I thought casually – a lift lobbyist who is out for large orders for his industry with cunningly chosen horror stories. He said that they should actually stop ten thousand lifts in Poland right away, and told me about the Polish grandma "who drags herself up six flights of stairs, because she doesn't trust the lift". He told me about a cleaning lady who was crushed inside a lift by her cleaning cart. "She was dead within an hour. That's why we're in favour of a regulation that double doors should be installed in all lifts." He was convinced that the managers of the lift corporation weren't aware of the price agreements. A couple of "idiots" amongst the salesmen had fallen for the temptation.

Enraged, he described the raid on 20 January 2004. "We had our board meeting at that point. They came around eight thirty, pulling out their ID cards. A professional hacker went on my computer. I asked him if he wanted me to give him my password. He said: no thanks, I'm already in."

Yes, my anonymous cartel hunter affirmed, the Commission hires specialists in "forensic IT". Quite quickly the companys' lawyers were there "and started bellowing in our ears about what we were not allowed to look at". You can find an astonishing amount of evidence under the search entry "confidential". The evidence is secured over night with the seal of the Commission. Meanwhile the offence of "Breaking Official Seals" was also punished, the German energy corporation EON had to pay thirty-eight million.

Back in the days, a graduate from the Commission's raid course told me, things sometimes went wrong. Once, the cartel hunters weren't discreet enough while entering a company. As soon as they had entered the lifts, the power was cut. I wasn't told whether that had happened to them in the lift cartel.

The African Commission

Since Staszek wasn't happy amongst Eurocrats, I came up with an idea for him, namely that he should start working for Gaddafi. It was a lucrative idea, Gaddafi had invested considerable amounts in the unification of Africa, and moreover, starting February 2009 he was President of the African Union for one year. Fifty-three member states, eight hundred million inhabitants – Gaddafi must need consultants from Brussels.

Excited, Staszek listened to me, but as of yet he hasn't gotten in touch with Gaddafi. He hesitated, hesitated about everything. He wanted to leave Brussels, however he didn't dare to risk the salary of six thousand and the life-long contract just yet. After a couple of months, he moved out of Mother Superior's place, only shaking his head at the thought of the cheerless orphanage. He got himself another bachelor pad, but lived there as if it was a hotel.

He also hesitated at another opportunity, and this one time I couldn't follow; this one time I couldn't understand him. We were sitting, as every so often, in the Congolese "La Callebasse" and had a cognac or two. Something was different than usual. Danielle, the Cameroon waitress with the proudly raised chin, sat down at our table, contrary to her usual habits. She had a bite on a chicken snack, her fingers shone with grease. After months of strict negligence the unthinkable happened; Danielle started to show interest in us. She went to top off the Congolese's glasses, we were sitting next to a group of indifferently swimming electric fish, and when Danielle came back to our table she loudly and firmly uttered the true but unexpected phrase: "Vous êtes cool." She, Danielle, to us, "you are cool"!

She asked about our lives. Selflessly, I told her I was a tourist in Brussels and hence passed the ball over to Staszek. He was not a tourist. Danielle turned to him. She didn't trouble herself with inconveniences. She told him which nights she was off and wrapped it up with the question: "Would you like to go out with me some time?" All the Last of the Mohicans from the Carpathian floodplains had to do was to name a day of the week. What did he do? He hesitated. Did he agree to anything? Nothing. I still can't believe it. Just in case Stay Sick comes to his senses, I will draft his job application to Gaddafi, as a precaution.

"Brother Leader of the Revolution!" I would start my letter according to Libyan custom, "my counsel isn't required by you anymore in many things. A 'Commission for the African Union' has already been founded, on which I would have advised you. I would have recommended providing a formidable building for the African

Commission, which has now already been done by the 'China State Construction Engineering Corporation'. A 99.9-metre high tower, a 30-metre high conference room, a grant from the Chinese government – the founding fathers of our humble confederation would have drooled over something like that.

Today it might appear to you as if our Valley of the Eurocrats is built for eternity. Sure, our capital is almost completely done; only the vertical glass egg of the European Council is missing. But how long that took! Just imagine, eight years after the signing of the Treaty of Rome did the European Commission only have three thousand two hundred civil servants, and twelve years went by before the Berlaymont was fully operational!

As an encouragement I should mention that, with some petrol dollars and customised advocacy, you will get your African unit in place much faster. You have the advantage of Addis Ababa being your fixed headquarters; Brussels is still struggling with Strasbourg and Luxemburg. I strongly recommend something like the Brusselian weather to you; the all-year-round equally divided cool weather advances the assiduity of the civil servants.

That was much plaudit, Brother Leader of the Revolution, now to the cadres. What annoys me on your homepage is the announcement of the prolongation of the application deadline for a new government body of the African Union because of absence of applicants. How could that be, how much are you paying? All you need is a motivated body of highly qualified and highly specialised civil servants, untroubled by material matters or elections. You could adopt the EU's remuneration system. There must be some appeal to VAT-free off-roaders.

Certainly, some of your heads of state will dawdle. You have to explain to them that elements of all powers are united in the European Commission: executive, legislative, jurisdiction. The guys know that from home, they will cheer with joy. Construct yourself an African Commission exactly like ours! Then the thing will run by itself.

In all fairness it needs to be said: Afrocrats will never be loved. Afrosceptical busybodies will object that the 'Pan-African Parliament' only has counselling authorities and that it is consigned to the South African backwater Midlands. Reply to them patiently that the African Union will be further democratised with every treaty amendment! Give the Pan-African Parliament an additional seat with full capacity, for example in Tripoli, and a general secretariat in Yaoundé!

The rest is just chippings from the plane of history. Brother Leader of the Revolution, 2009 was the fortieth anniversary of your seize of power, you're certainly thinking about your entry in the history books. Do like we do, that's my advice. Maybe the glory of immortality awaits you. At least a roundabout will be named after you, as with Robert Schuman in Brussels."

The Muslims

If I wanted to talk about the Islamisation of Brussels I could just recite statistics. More than a quarter of all Brusselians are Muslim, more than half of the newborns are born into Muslim families, the most popular first name since 2001 is Mohammed. However, I could also talk about Hamed. Hamed was a hip-hop dancer. Today, he doesn't dance anymore.

Long did I put off my venture into the Islam of the European capital. An intersection in the Moroccan neighbourhood of Anderlecht was the only place in the world where I had ever been threatened with violence. Finally, I got myself together and started my research. I visited one of the most religious and one of the most irreligious Muslims in the city. The courteously composed theologian Mustafa, and the cordially hyperactive hip-hop dancer Said.

Nowhere else do EU and Islam get so close as in the Grande Mosquée. Established as an Orient pavilion for the World Exhibition in 1897, the "Great Mosque" is in fact a mosque today. Four Maghrebian imams work in the model building, along with a Saudi Arabian, an Egyptian, a Turkish and an Albanian imam. Every Friday at two o'clock, eight hundred white-dressed believers stream towards the place. They stream through the canyon of offices in Gotham City.

I asked the imam from Morocco, Mustafa, if the scantily clad female European joggers who run through "Jubelpark" close by his mosque didn't bother him. No, he replied with a tiny smile. He called it an advantage that the mosque wasn't situated in a Muslim neighbourhood. He was responsible for the converts and had already dealt with a couple of Eurocrats who had converted to Islam. "Most of them don't let that show in their workplaces, they are scared of negative reactions."

We took off our shoes and the imam showed me into the great hall. A couple of men were kneeling on the wall-to-wall carpet, deep in prayer. Barely audible murmurs, the whirring of electric fans, slow movements, peace. Some were sitting, leaning idly against pillars. "They are meditating", the imam explained. In the middle of the room, a stout muezzin stood up and took his place. The imam showed me the enthroned pulpit on top of wooden stairs, from where he was preaching on Fridays; the better part of the only thirty-five minute long Friday prayer is appointed to the sermon. He said that he addressed issues like the caricature conflict in his sermons. It might happen that a sermoniser added fuel to the fire in one of the eighty mosques in Brussels. He, on the other hand, tries to instil calm. He promotes interfaith dialogue trough the extensive event programme of the Great Mosque.

The day after, the hip-hop dancer Said took me through Anderlecht. He was over thirty, was known in the hip-hop scene as "old school", wore Adidas gear from the seventies. He did indeed possess the traditional white Friday robe, but barely ever went to the mosque. He had very little contact with his religious father, was married to a non-Muslim woman from Haiti, and came down from the adrenalin rush from dancing by smoking weed. Luckily, he drove slowly, since his gestures at the steering wheel weren't dissimilar to break-dancing. The question about Islam stirred him up, because his mate Hamed doesn't dance anymore. Hamed, Said told me, had consulted five imams. Not one of them had directly forbidden him to dance "but one said to Hamed: dancing is not good". Hamed concluded that it would contradict the spirit of Islam to promote himself publicly. Said on the other hand, lived off public appearances.

We sat down in the tiny garden of his ground floor flat, his wife carried out their little son Sahel. Sahel means "easy" in Arabic, however the young father was hard on himself. "What I'm doing", escaped his lips, "is actually worse than what Hamed has done. I even bring children into the dancing!" He was going to keep on dancing though, he said decidedly with an equally proud as unsettled look. Hamed only dances at home now.

The Children

In August, or so I was told, the Brusselian Europe machine is shut down to emergency operation. I decided on a radical change of programme and spent three days roaming the city with children. Childless myself, I was at loss with this task: what do you do with kids in a narrow, crowded conference city like Brussels?

The children were my two nephews from the Lower Austrian countryside. The older one was seven, the younger four years old. Their mom was there as well.

Our hotel was situated in the Molenbeek street "Little Anatolia", there was barely anything but Turkish pizzerias there. In the morning we went to the street market. My nephews were wearing their Spiderman jackets to protect them from the coolness of the Belgian midsummer. Maybe it was because of the boys' bright blond hair, maybe because of the spider web-shaped rubber pattern on the jackets, in any case a young curly-haired Turkish girl started to grope the older one as we walked through the crowd. Amused, the girl laughed, the older boy turned away irritably. Mum had brought the Spiderman jackets from her holidays in Turkey.

But what to do with kids? Kids' museum, chocolate museum, Bruparck? My nephews are growing up in the country, they are almost exclusively transported in private cars, therefore unfamiliar public transports were reliable attractions. The first flight of their lives; and then to be served a hotdog on the aeroplane. The Métro, in which the older one curiously turned his head and the little one kept quiet; dumbfounded. The lift in the central pillar of the Atomium, with a view into the shaft.

Trains, lifts, escalators, moving walkways. And the double-decker sightseeing bus. We all got headphones, and the boys listened patiently to the entire cassette, even to the praise of the Belgian educational system, reeled off in the forty-percent-unemployment zone by the "Kanal".

The fact that the Belgians have a King with two castles the boys found quite impressive. They frolicked about with much enthusiasm on the moist sand of the little island, created before their eyes by the receding North Sea. There, on the outskirts of Ostend, I unintentionally caused them mirth on my own accord. I swam a bit along the shore and even though it was a public beach, a red-clad "redder" from the West-Flemish provincial government blew his whistle ordering me to come back. Too late did I realise that the lifeguard's tooting and waving was intended for me. The boys had realised before me.

In the evening, back in the Little Anatolia of Brussels, there was suddenly a ball. The ball belonged to a small

Turkish boy who was watched over by an old Bulgarian-Turkish woman, "for money", as she emphasised. Suddenly, my nephews were playing football. I could characterise the scene on the poor church plain as a heart-warming multicultural unity, for which the magic spell of football was responsible. At the same time I must maintain that the fouls outweighed the conventional moves. The three boys shouted at each other in their respective languages. After every dribbling the Turkish boy changed sports and performed karate-like movements. If my nephews would try to get the ball, he would gladly beat them for it. "Mum, he's crazy!" my youngest nephew shouted. And then punched back.

At some point, I will ask the boys what they really thought of their holiday in the capital. In Brussels itself they made contradictory comments. The older one didn't have time to answer; he had to look, look, look. "It's a totally ugly country", the younger one told me inside the windowless snack bar inside the Atomium. Shortly after, when he got his ice cream, he revised his verdict to "totally cosy".

Maybe later, the boys will say that Brussels wasn't that different from home, from home in the Lower Austrian village. The pizzeria was Turkish, like at home. And the children were Turkish, just like in the playground at home.

The Chinese

A spectre is haunting Europe – a spectre called G2. G2 signifies that the US and China are ruling the world together, without the EU. It was assumed that China was advancing even faster in the crisis as before. As the West was crumbling, China was growing substantially. I started to wonder: should we all learn Chinese?

A Brusselian interpreter prodded me to the subject. She spoke of a secret programme of the European Commission. The interpreters of the People's Republic of China would translate according to the selective demands of their leaders; the EU was therefore training their own Chinese interpreters.

Maybe I shouldn't have believed the interpreter. The five hundred salaried and two thousand seven hundred freelancing interpreters constitute a specific tribe in the Eurocrat valley. They are a nervous, imbalanced folk in need of peace and quiet; their heads are haunted by 135,000 days a year of interpreting technical terms.

I went to the Crowne Plaza, to a "policy dialogue" EU–China. It was merely announced that the ambassador of China to the EU was there, and the congestion reminded me of Noah's Ark. At exactly ten thirty the door was closed, the Chinese ambassador wanted to speak uninterrupted by latecomers. The lockout of signed-in participants created a feeling of a hierarchic, authoritative, outdated China. Shortly after I got to experience dynamic China.

Yin Zonghua, the embassy's economy expert with colourful space bubbles on his tie, looked like a bureaucrat. Then he got started, speaking freely, with the racy wit of a sales rep. He addressed the listeners as "distinguished think-tank tank-thinkers". Just like the polite Commission officials, he rattled through the win-win numbers of the third greatest economy of the world. "Don't take my numbers too seriously", he humorously qualified, "I only recently finished my PhD." The European accusation, of China dumping too much and protecting the climate too little, he disbanded with one single joke: "Chinese bicycles could help you attaining the climate objectives. They only are a third of the price." He closed with the words: "China welcomes you."

The second part was about climate protection; many people left the room. A young Chinese girl, student at the College of Europe in Bruges, took the floor towards the end. I heard her say "impotence" several times. Impotence, impotence, impotence; the male Carrie Bradshaw twitched. The Chinese student did however mean "importance". She posed three questions. She asked eagerly, however her questions about the importance of this and that were completely general. There it was again, outdated China.

I gave it a try and took one hour of Chinese. My teacher was Dinah, a small dainty woman from Brussels; her eyebrows were merely short thin lines. She studied Chinese translation, no university in Brussels offered interpreting. She had started out with sixty classmates, in her fourth year only thirteen were left. "Half of them quit because they realise that they will never comprehend Chinese." I learned that Chinese has no declinations, no genders, no conjugations, but five pitches and ten sibilants. The writing, however, tells stories. A "woman" under a "roof" means "peace". The idea is, with a woman at home, the man has his peace.

Dinah had spent four years swotting frantically. Now she startled me with the statement that she would hardly find a job in Europe. She had studied one term in China and saw her professional outlooks to be more promising there. "Since I know Chinese, I was treated like a princess in China. That was a great feeling." Off to China, that almost sounded catchy. A Chinese man wasn't what Dinah wanted however. She preferred Brits. "Chinese men are not romantic whatsoever."

I went to the Chinese department of the European Commission. A German woman and an Irishman saw me in, they had nametags with Chinese characters, the Irishman had adopted a Chinese baby. I asked about the secret programme. The secret crumbled into an EU-promoted term of studies in China for then up to eight European interpreting students, most of whom had just failed their courses. Yes, we should learn Chinese. However, before we do, we have to work. Work on our love for China.

The Churches

Disgust, that was what brought me to the Netherlands for the first time. Animal rights activist killing politician, Islamist murdering filmmaker, court approving gassing of geese, representative with angelic face chasing the pope in a BMW sports car. Further, I read that the Dutch are selling their churches on a large scale, turning them into discos or mosques. Could be that I might come across as old-fashioned. The Carrie Bradshaw in me took a break; the convent school pupil hidden underneath was distraught. I didn't find it normal to sell churches.

I got in touch with the specialist company "Reliplan" and took off, anticipating Dutch perversions. At Zwijndrecht train station, pronounced "swine-drecht", the senior manager of Reliplan received me. Mickey Bosschert was a deft and chubby, modern and motherly sixty-year-old businesswoman clad in light colours. Her first word made me suspicious. "Grüßgott!" – "God bless!" Was the legendary European church saleswoman trying to provoke me? "Why did you say 'Grüßgott' to me?" I asked her.

"That's what you say in Austria, right?" she replied. Forty years earlier, while being a student, she had worked at a Viennese hotel. After that she had become an entrepreneur and made millions in cosmetics. In the early nineties she founded Reliplan.

Ms Bosschert started by saying: "I have already sold nine hundred churches." That meant that she consulted parishes over years and explored possibilities of potential utilisation. "Consulting with the churches takes a long time", she said, "they always argue." She said it was "nice" that the parishes of reformed communities were allowed to sell their churches independently. The topic was "delicate" and "difficult" to raise with the Catholic Church. The bishopric decides amongst the Catholics, and many a bishop prefers demolition to desecration.

Some hundred churches had become residential houses. A picturesque convent in the Ardennes was reconstructed into a holiday home. Not all Christian communities sold churches, a small minority of strict reformists were countering and even bought churches from the liberal communities. Ms Bosschert didn't want supermarkets as clients anymore; that was met with refusal. Three churches had been turned into mosques, that she wouldn't do anymore either. When people see mosques where their churches used to be, she said, "they weep at the walls".

I had ended up with the absolute manager of church sales. "Once, I told my husband that now I had everything, except a Native American. Next day, a Native American was standing in my office and was looking for a chapel." She added that the American Indian client had caused her some trouble. The Indians danced at night dressed in white robes and refreshed themselves with animating liquids. The neighbours didn't appreciate that.

She took me to the former Ichutuskerk in Zwijndrecht, built by a famous architect. "This one was difficult to sell." A pyramid-shaped roof took up ninety percent of the space, which couldn't be altered. I had entered a day-care centre. The hallway was designed in a friendly fashion with flamingos, flying fish, plastic palm trees. A monkey was lying in a hammock, banana in hand, sunglasses on.

It was explained to me that ten week-old "bebies" could already be admitted to this private service provider, from early morning until seven at night. The laundry room was installed in the centre of the former house of prayer. In 1999, the organ was sold, in 2001, the day-care centre moved in. No one could tell me where the entrance to the church, nor where the altar had once been.

I asked Ms Bosschert to show me a church currently for sale. Her pretty Indonesian colleague drove us through the southern Dutch motorway-land, but we couldn't get a hold of any sacristan. We sat down in a motorway restaurant. There Ms Bosschert told me why she did it. Certainly, the church sales were booming. "Within the next years or so, two thousand churches will be available in the Netherlands alone. No such thing as recession. It gets better for us."

The beginning, however, was something else. Ms Bosschert had lost her daughter to a disease. She had stopped working and gone looking for comfort in a church. The pastor had told her that she wanted to demolish the church. "I thought that was a pity." Ms Bosschert had that church renovated, just like many other churches. You could say that she had committed herself to the rescue of churches. In this moment, I found the Dutch woman almost normal.

The Christians

In the autumn of 2009, I once again tried to track down people who were doing things for the Christian cause in the European bubble. I had been unsuccessful during my reconstruction of the Rocco case. Brussels is strictly secular. Any reminder of Jesus Christ had been obliterated from the poster hanging on the bridge over rue Belliard during Christmas-time. "Merry Christmas" would have been too scandalous, therefore people were congratulated on a not otherwise specified season with "Season Greetings".

Just the fact that I was looking for a Catholic lobby made for irritation in Brussels' environment. "What do the Catholics need a lobby for!" a reporter for a Conservative newspaper called out. Sure, the appropriate demeanour of the Church is open for dispute. If you ask me, I would say that at least the good Lord would need a lobby in Brussels.

Once again, it was the same thing. COMECE, the Brusselian representation of the European Episcopal Conference, equipped with a significant number of personnel, didn't react to my numerous knockings. Devoted or abdicated, who knows? Once again, there were no Poles willing to rescue Europe. It seemed to me that only an elder Anglican was following the European legislation procedure actively. The Anglican was difficult to get a hold of; he wore himself out travelling between England, Brussels and Strasbourg.

In this bleak situation, a call reached me from the country to which I had moved in 2004 – Slovakia. The Slovakian representative in the European Commission had just gone back to Slovakian politics, thus a Slovakian newspaper requested information about his Brusselian workings. On the one hand that was appropriate; Ján Figel was regarded as the most faithful Catholic in the resigning Commission. On the other hand, there was nothing to be said about Figel. I had never heard anyone talk about his work.

I made enquiries about the man. I heard that he was "decent", "smart", "sincere", "pleasant", "kind". He seemed likeable to me as well, when I saw him eating modestly in the Commission's cafeteria at lunchtime. A former employee of the Franciscan order told me that Figel had secretly helped a couple of Christian organisations. Some complained about the Slovak's avoidance of conflicts. When there was the need for a department for the newly joined Romanians in 2007, people took from the Commissioner with the most Christian humility. Figel had to give up his "Multilingualism" authority. He didn't object.

My topic – Christianity in the Valley of the Eurocrats – dulled me. I had been catapulted out of the ludicrously speedy communication channels of the Green-Liberals' central environment before the rusty mills of God. I needed reconciliation; I went to a private party. The guests were what Staszek used only as a peevishly thrown-out swearword, "expats". Many were active around the European institutions. I didn't know these people. Surprisingly enough, I ended up amongst Christians, amongst active members of an English-speaking Baptist community. I learned about the Baptists that they were nice, that their church was situated in a suburb, that they lived in the suburbs and that they went home at eleven o'clock on Saturday nights.

The Baptist hostess was celebrating her thirtieth birthday; towards midnight she considered breaking up the party. Then, an attractive couple arrived with motorcycle helmets under their arms, an athletic model Teuton and his tall girlfriend. She wasn't a Baptist, but she was Slovakian, and this coincidence bestowed me my most biblical moment in Brussels.

The young woman was a true Slovakian beauty, with blond hair and brown eyes. I asked her in Slovakian: "What is a good Mid-Slovakian girl like you doing in a city like this?" The skilled small talker was confused. She was thrown off track for a moment by the sudden possibility to speak her mother tongue. She stopped short. She swallowed. Then she replied with a movingly simple phrase in Slovakian: "I work for bad people."

She worked for the Russian monopoly company Gasprom, as an employee at a well-known Brusselian lobby for hire; even Microsoft was one of their clients. The moving moment was brief, other guests came in and everyone settled again on this uniform expat-English, where everything was "very good" and there was no Fall of Mankind. Now the Slovakian was once again describing her work in a normal manner, as "consultancy", her employers were good to her. But I had heard it. I had heard it and had seen the shamed glance in her hazelnut eyes. The Baptists were already sleeping at this point. Just suppose, there is good and evil. Just suppose, there are fallen girls, and suppose, a fallen girl wanted to convert herself. Who would take her hand?

The Italians

Souvenir du Pays noir" is written on an old postcard, "souvenir of the black country". The photos show a sooty landscape with coalmines, chimneys, barges, wagons, barracks. Men's faces black from dirt, silently telling of the "fight for coal", when Belgium could boost their ruined economy after the Second World War with just coal. In between, a picture of fleet-footed Italianità: men in extraordinarily elegant suits playing bocce. In the foreground, a bellied demijohn with wine, in the background a pointy mountain of dark-grey debris. From the coal spoil tip, called "terril" in French, a couple of lost little saplings stick out.

As I turned my attention to Brussels' Italians, it didn't have to be to the two thousand six hundred Italian Commission officials. The Italian element is deeply rooted in Belgium, in the French-speaking part some ten percent originate from Italian families. The artist Alessia belongs to them on her mother's side. Fifty thousand Italians came to the country as miners, as a result of the Belgian-Italian national treaty from 1946. Back then, they came in chartered trains, a thousand every week.

The Belgian secret police struck previous convicts and communists off the list. Once in Belgium, the enlisted workers were sent into the mines without any training. The following day some refused to go back down. They were then taken away by the police to the Brusselian "petit château" and detained, then deported. "Everyone will die like rats, since there is no emergency exit", a father said to his child back then. On 8 August 1956 it happened, on 8 August 1956, they died like rats.

Later, many Italians left the declining Walloon mining towns and moved to Brussels. I wanted to get to know some of them. I called Alessia; we hadn't seen each other for a while. In the meantime she had acted out numerous possibilities of having another life, only to discard them immediately after. She made no documentary about fear of dentists and death, she had opened no night bar with a partner, she had not taken that bread-and-butter job in the theatre's ticket office. Now she was applying for social credit so she could open her own breakfast café.

Alessia had wrinkled her nose at my screening of the Eurocrats, now she was interested. It was a Sunday afternoon; she invited me over right away. She was staying in a different flat, was momentarily visiting an old Flemish friend. Both of them had probably had a couple of drinks; the aroma of spirits was spread out through the dark panelled room. A sexual vibe, impalpable and indefinable, was in the air.

I posed my question. Lo and behold, both of them had had Italian miners in their families. Proud as a wild steed, Alessia told us about her grandfather. "He had grains in his skin, his lungs were corroded from brimstone, but he was so unbelievably proud!" Once, her grandfather had reached inside the desk drawer, pulled out a piece of coal and announced to his granddaughters with a croaking voice: "I dug this up."

The grandfather was long dead; Alessia arranged a meeting with her uncle Filippo, born in Sicily in 1938, already acting like a bourgeois Belgian. He still went to the Laekenian old gentlemen's club "L'Isola", however already listened to the French mass. I met with Filippo in Alessia's flat. She had cleaned, and even though she had partied until the morning she posed as the exemplary niece. The uncle spoke to me in great detail, Alessia tried really hard but soon lost the plot, soon became bored by the Italian family saga after all.

"We were suffering from hunger in Sicily", Filippo told me. He had often eaten carob pods and thistles in order to survive. Then there was a recruitment poster from the Belgian government hanging on the town hall of Enna. "The Belgians promised us a small house. That turned out to be a barrack in which German war prisoners had formerly been detained."

No, not even the Belgians were fair to their foreign workers: "If you don't like it, macaroni, then go back!" Filippo was fourteen when he descended eight hundred metres for the first time, initially with his father. He was afraid;

an Italian friend had died, flushed away by ground water. Filippo got away from mining work at the age of nineteen, but said self-confidently: "I was strong and could do the work of adults. I earned twenty francs more since I went there alone before the crack of dawn, for control work."

I went to Charleroi, to the Marcinelle district, to the former Black Country. In 1955, the fight for coal had successfully hit a production record, on 8 August the following year a fire broke out in the "Bois du Cazier" mine. As late as 23 August, the rescue team finally managed to penetrate the 1,035 metres deep shaft. Beneath, everything was quiet. The one who reported to the surface only had two words to say. "Tutti cadaveri." 136 of the 262 dead were Italians.

Bois du Cazier is a museum today. A half-round rusty-red metal tunnel is to be seen of the module "Nissen Hut", in which many Italians lived at first. You can see the dressing room, which is called "room of the hanged" because of the gear hanging on hoisted hooks. You can read that stricter safety regulations were issued by the European Coal and Steel Community, the genesis for the EU, because of what happened at Marcinelle. Before Marcinelle, two thousand men died underground, in the years after Marcinelle, twenty. Even when there were no bocce-playing men I could barely turn my eyes from the grey spoil tips. He had been playing on the spoil tip at home when he was a boy, Filippo told me, together with Polish boys. Cherry trees were growing on the tip. I didn't wish Filippo's childhood on any child. But that he had played on a mountain that his father had built – for that I envied him a little.

The Soviet Union

"The EU is the new Soviet Union", Staszek often said. I retorted just as often: "If that's true, then you're in on it too." Anyway, he inspired me to compare the two entities with each other.

To begin with, I tried an aesthetic comparison. I couldn't find an equivalent in the EU to the praised art of early Soviet propaganda posters. I did discover something in a later period, on the Soviet posters from the sixties, when the Communist ideology spread out in the young nations of the Third World. The harmless multikulti-style of this time definitely resembled the countless websites of the European Commission. Both systems' creations employ laughing children, one white child with blond hair, one white child with dark hair, as well as an African and an Asian child. And it's ever so bright.

In June 2009, a former member of the politburo from the CPSU was elected to the European Parliament. That announcement inspired me; I had to get to know the elder gentleman. Who, if not him, could compare the two unions from a more intimate perspective? In September, I went to visit him.

His assistant already differed from the fifteen hundred young and dynamic assistants defining work in the European Parliament. Anatoly could be called mature at least; he had a bit of a belly. The delegate himself, seventy-four years old, expected me in his office sitting bolt upright. Nothing gave away anything about this Alfrēds Rubiks in the close to empty space. The nice narrow divan he had taken over from his Italian predecessor. Rubiks said that he never lay down on the divan.

"I would rather act in Latvia", the ethnic Latvian said. In Latvia, his political practice authorities had been banned however, so from 1991 to 1997 he had even been imprisoned in autonomous Latvia, accused for an attempted coup. He gave me his book written in Russian, in which he demanded recognition of his innocence. Had he been sent to prison guilty or innocent? A political question, I hadn't dug very deep into his case. In such cases, people have to make decisions based on instinct. I addressed the man, who still called himself a Communist, like an innocent.

We spoke Russian and began comparing the "Sovetsky Soyuz" with the "Evropeisky Soyuz". He commented on my aesthetic observation with the words that the Soviet posters had contained "more humanism". The comparison between the Supreme Soviet and the European Parliament I soon found ineffective. The Soviet Parliament only met twice a year, while the European equivalent, being the most conference-happy chamber in the world, met in forty-four weeks of sessions per year. The parallels between the Soviet State Planning Committee "Gosplan" and the European Commission seemed more astounding. Gosplan planned for up to twenty years into the future, the White Papers of the Commission also reach far beyond legislation periods.

But how, Alfrēds Petrovich, how was it in the politburo? He said that the "first secretaries" from the fifteen Soviet republics of his time assembled there at the time. Even the editor in chief for *Pravda* had been a member, the *Financial Times* in Brussels didn't formally have this status just yet. The politburo met every week; the European Council falls behind. Rubiks described the fact that everyone could speak Russian in the politburo as a "big plus". There were no interpreters present. He criticised the "Americanisation" and "Anglicisation" of Europe, ninety percent of all unofficial meetings were held in English. He was forced to anglicise himself now, a well-thumbed English-Latvian pocket dictionary lay next to his computer.

Every now and then, the assistant Anatoly looked through the door urgingly. He feared that I was exhausting the old man. Rubiks however, had become quite animated by our topic. He said that I should come back in six months, by then he would know the EU much better.

He called the EU a "grand bureaucratic machine", processes in the Soviet Union had been much more efficient.

"If the EU continues on like this", he added, "it will fall apart by 2015." I asked him if he had been able to foretell the end of the Soviet Union at the time. He said no. "There were no indications for that."

The Llamas and the Fat Cats

My only reason for flying to Ireland was that the 0.8 percent of the EU population lived there, who were still being consulted concerning European treaties. A feeling crept over me in Brussels that no nation was to be consulted about Europe for a long time. All the more urgently did I want to experience the second Irish Lisbon Treaty referendum.

I was never particularly drawn to the Green Island. It was my first visit. I wasn't exactly enchanted. My verdict probably turned out so harsh because I had come directly from Switzerland. Ireland is the most expensive country in the euro zone, the Swiss Press warned me, the country isn't even cheap for the Swiss. Involuntarily, I started to compare. Disregarding the pub culture at best, Ireland didn't attain the quality of life in Switzerland in any aspect. Astonished, I observed that the Irish train travellers had to stand in long rows on the platform after buying their tickets, along high metal fences. Only with the permission of the authorities were they allowed aboard the train.

Then, the food. With a lot of money you could get lucky. There was grub in the Irish fast-food chains, which made me long for the delicacies of McDonald's. "Fish & chips" in the pub; the fish tasteless and watery, the chips with a bouquet of engine oil. Better not to look for a café for breakfast. An apple pie for five euros, mostly composed of a thick hard crust.

Finally, the sight of the Irish real estate. Much had been heard about it; prices had gone up between 2000 and 2008 by three hundred percent. The bubble had popped; the government debt was to be quadrupled from 2007 to 2013. The sight of the houses was a fright, still the ancient poverty of the Irish was screaming out from them. Everywhere fences and walls, the high grey walls kept the sunlight out of the tiny gardens. Incredulously, I pressed my nose against the window display of a real estate agent: 370,000 euros for a small low petty bourgeois shack in the countryside? How much had the salesman asked for before the crisis? Is that what the "Celtic Tiger" looked like, one of the richest countries in Europe? Or had that only been statistics?

I had flown to Ireland for six euros with the budget airline Ryanair, I paid more for every additional Irish purchase I made. Seen during the bus ride between Shannon and Galway, the Irish countryside was pretty as a postcard. The pastures surrounded by picturesque stonewalls were evergreen under the hermetic cloudy sky. As long as there were no houses to be seen, it was beautiful. Almost as a proof of the mild climate, palm trees were planted in front of some western Irish houses. Sure, the Gulf Stream kept the palm trees from freezing. I would however not say that the palm trees were thriving. These palm trees, puny and limited to a couple of metres in height, fitted nicely to the properties.

Nevertheless, the Irish did look after European democracy once more on 2 October 2009. Once contested by a complaining citizen, since 1987 every European treaty was subject to a referendum in Ireland: the Single European Act, Maastricht, Amsterdam, Nice times two, Lisbon times two. After the rejection in 2008, the assembled establishment of the republic fought in 2009 for a yes. Companies like Ryanair and Intel made up full-page advertisements for the Lisbon Treaty. On a flyer of a leftist Treaty opponent, I found a nice expression describing the yes-sponsors: "Fat Cats".

I came to Galway the day before the ballot. Other news was already becoming the story of the day: a tsunami in Indonesia; a queue of six hundred unemployed before the commercial chain Marks & Spencer, which was only looking for a couple of extras to help out during the Christmas dealings; five llamas had run away from a circus and were blocking the Dublin Circular Road.

I went to the same pub in Galway three times: before the ballot, during and the day after. Amongst the men the conversation mostly involved the national sovereignty or "what Europe had done for Ireland". A young teacher explained the Irish soul to me deep into the night. The Irish would only talk in pubs, he claimed, lunch was to be had in silence. It had to do with the trauma of the great famine. The hundreds of years of poverty were also responsible for the Irish being "obsessed with owning property".

When I spoke to the women they always expressed their worry that the sons of Ireland could be pulled into a foreign army against their will. A young woman advised me "not to shop and drink". She had gone shopping and drinking and had missed going to the polling place. She took a long time putting on her pullover. "The Lisbon Treaty is false", she said meanwhile, "niente". Most of my conversation partners wanted to vote no. Yet when the national broadcaster started reporting at eleven o'clock the following day, the yes was already set. Already two months later, on 1 December 2009, the Lisbon Treaty became the new constitutional law of the European Union.

On the day of the ballot count I went to Dublin. The first thing I noticed about the capital was the queue on the platform, this time squeezed in between a metal fence and a plexiglas wall. In the evening I went to the Hilton, to the big victory party of the yes-campaign. "Ireland for Europe" and "Generation Yes" were both there, many young people with relations to Brussels. I had never before seen so many euphoric Eurocrats, yet even in a moment of happiness the familiar opinions announced themselves. An Irishman from "Europe for Ireland" demanded a definite smoking ban in Brusselian cafés. Without me even having mentioned the subject, he started ranting about the pavements in Brussels.

An Irish civil servant started to loosen up. For two years, he had maintained the same assertions for the Irish.

Now he said it would be funny if the President of the Commission would announce on Monday: "Thank you for the yes, we will now start drafting the conscripts. And abortion is binding, retroactive for five years."

A young redhead Commission official took my breath away for a brief moment. The German woman explicitly praised the way the Irish railways forced their travellers to stand in lines on the platform. "That should be introduced in Germany as well. In Germany, boarding a train is pure chaos. That's why there are hundreds of casualties every year."

At the peak of the party, the leader of the yes-campaign made a speech. Pat Cox, former President of the European Parliament, currently communication consultant to the Commissioner for Consumer Protection, advisor to Michelin, Pfizer and Microsoft, and amicably attached to the Brusselian lobby firm APCO. Wait a minute, I thought, isn't he the fattest of all cats? The speech by Fat Cat Pat was fiery. The campaign had swept over the country "like a tsunami", he said. "It was as if the soul of our nation" had been on trial.

The second piece of news that weekend was that the llamas had gone missing anew. They had been taken from the motorway the previous day and put in an enclosure of the Dublin municipality. Now they were gone again. This time they had also been joined by a couple of goats. The Irish, on the other hand, only said no to the Lisbon Treaty once. The second time around they let themselves be snared by fat cats.

The Boredom

This chapter is boring. It's composed of a ruthless enumeration of treaty breaches, which on one single day were noticed by the European Commission. On this randomly chosen workday, a total of fifty-six MS were exhorted. In Brussels, MS doesn't stand for multiple sclerosis; it means Member State. The Commission is the custodian of the treaties. It sees everything, like a pedantic governess.

The first warning is called "letter of formal notice", after that the MS has two months to reply. The second warning is already the final one; it's quite harmlessly called "reasoned opinion". After two additional months, the MS is remitted to the European Court of Justice. I found the official statements IP/09/1438–1492 in the Commission's press room, in which I could still smell smoke five months after the fire. Now to the enumeration. For the sake of fairness, I would first like to say that only at the end of this chapter a person will be mentioned briefly.

On 8 October 2009, the Commission warned that twenty-one MS weren't implementing the liberalisation of the rail transport sufficiently enough. MS Greece wasn't allowing carriers and the fuel merchants any establishment freedom and didn't set up any independent aviation authorities. A presidential decree restrained the voting rights of non-governmental bondholders of an energy supplier to five percent; the Greek automobile society charged their members value added tax on roadway repair services. MS Spain was neglecting governmental procurements, let a company from the Valencia region award public contracts, was at that very place leading outlet water into a nature reserve and had inconsistent value added tax rules for travel agencies.

The Scottish city Glasgow didn't advertise their social housing, the Dutch city Eindhoven developed the site for a community centre without a call for proposals, the Italian province Sondrio only gave low-cost housing to students with an Italian address or passport. Marks & Spencer couldn't skim the tax abatement in Great Britain designated to attained loss abroad; Belgium breached the "Limosa declaration". Bulgaria built ski-lifts in bird sanctuaries, Romania established undersized sanctuaries for wild birds. Luxembourg and Portugal protracted the recognition of Bulgarian and Romanian professional qualifications; Luxembourg didn't give their nurses a training that complied with the minimum standard.

MS Austria granted a too broad value added tax exception on sports related services and incorporated standard consumption tax into the compulsory value added tax obligation contrary to the guidelines. Slovakia and the Czech Republic insufficiently protected costumers against unfair contracts. In Portugal and Cyprus, non-native real estate agents were being discriminated against, moreover, in Portugal patent agents and solicitors as well. Belgium discriminated regarding transit of domestic gas, the Netherlands when giving out foreign exchange scholarships, Finland regarding value added tax, Slovakia regarding legal advice during the construction of a highway, Greece regarding the carrier services and veterinarians, Hungary and Latvia regarding airport ground operations.

On 8 October 2009, the governess surely was having a good day. In her defence, it should be added that not only fifty-six MS were reprimanded in total, but also actions were dismissed against nine MS on the same day. That evening, I met one of these multilingual brainiacs who were intellectually and sexually bored of Brussels. Liliana had in the meantime made it into the last round of the Concours; her chances of getting hired as a civil servant were promising. I read her the statements of the day out loud. "You will work for this specialty within world history", I shouted euphorically, "for this Leviathan, for this unprecedented fickle thing between authority, government and Last Judgment!" She smiled tiredly.

I took the Romanian intellectual to Saint Gilles, to the "Brasserie Verschueren". When the greying waiter approached us I whispered to her that she had just now been served a spinach soup by Belgium's most famous terrorist. Naturally, I had gotten this information from Alessia. The man had blown up some bank and had gone to prison for it. The bored Liliana found that briefly entertaining. Personally, I think it's more exciting that something like the European Commission even exists.

The Refuge

She wouldn't have wanted me to tell her story. So let's leave out her name, her appearances, her home country. I ask her for forgiveness for not keeping her story to myself. In Brusselian terms, it's unusually existential. It deeply moved me.

The young woman is a political scientist. Her father teaches at a university, although she maintains in a credible manner that she wasn't raised with a silver spoon in her mouth. She acts neither snobbish nor elitist, there's even something provincial about her. For a couple of years she lived outside her home country, in Ireland. There, she wrote an analytical thesis about an attempt of the Irish government to explain the European constitution of the time to the Irish people in podium discussions. The young political scientist speaks excellent English. I noticed that she always said "yeah, yeah, yeah" as a confirmation during conversations in English; always three times. I thought that was how you do it.

When the crisis hit Ireland, harder than any other western European country, she was working in an uninteresting office job in Dublin. She breaks up with her Irish boyfriend who doesn't accept this and starts stalking her. He goes behind her back to her home country, visits her parents, beseeching them. He sends greetings to her from the church where she was baptised. The ex is related to one of the most powerful men in Ireland. He doesn't leave her alone; the foreign girl is scared. Winter comes. At the end of an uninteresting day at the office, she goes home, seven hundred fifty euros for an unheated chamber. A black crow sits in her room. The black crow, which has slipped inside through the fireplace, looks at the woman like a trespasser.

I got to know the young political scientist in Brussels. She was extremely happy to be there, Brussels was her refuge. Brussels' European bubble was actually growing as the rest of Europe was crumbling. The Lisbon Treaty advanced that growth; the supply of input for the upgraded European Parliament alone should mean work for hundreds of lobbyist bodies. My trusted tobacco lobbyist meanwhile sensed that the health subject would come to Brussels. He was already looking for costumers within this business not yet established in Brussels.

The young political scientist immediately got a job in Brussels, her Irish study opened doors for her. Her new employer couldn't have read the middle part of the study in which the political scientist applies her valued philosopher Habermas to the Irish EU constitution podiums. The "ideal speech situation" compared to the rigid EU briefing divided into two-minute statements in the Irish countryside – that was truly rock hard reading. As is common practice in Brussels, these Irish podium discussions were short. The Homo Brusselian is constantly moving in such tight time frames. This scares off the simple citizen. For the Irishwoman, who is in want of mammograms in the western Irish hospitals, or for the Irishman, who is moved by the Atlantic Ocean depleted of fish, that was nothing.

Once she arrived in Brussels, the Brusselian job astonished the young political scientist. She worked for a big company that created advertising exclusively for the European institutions, but mostly there were only Excel charts to be filled out. At the end of one workday, she's called in to see her manager. There was probably an Excel chart filled out incorrectly, she thinks. And she's let go. She's still on her trial period, term of notice one week. The manager excuses her from her last days, she goes to her desk, packs up her things, and doesn't need to come back ever again.

Once again, she's scared for her life. She spends her summer being anxious. Then she's saved once again. Thanks to her Irish study, never read by anyone, she gets a temporary job at the European Commission. I met her on the evening of her first day during a reception. She said that there was no expiration date on this temporary position, "at the end of the month I could already be unemployed again". At eight thirty, she only spoke about needing to go to bed. "I can't allow myself to make any more mistakes." Her story hadn't yet come to an end; she was living in a European precarity. Whether she eventually found her final refuge, the lifelong guaranteed civil servant position at the European Commission? I really hope so. She's a sincere person.

The only thing that really irritated me was that she always exclaimed "yeah, yeah, yeah" while listening to someone. One time she was conversing with an English native speaker, and I overheard them speaking. I heard that the native speaker also uttered scattered yeahs as he was listening. At times he said "yeah", at times "yeah, yeah", at times even "yeah, yeah, yeah". The young political scientist does everything right. Maybe she just agrees a little too often.

On Holiday

As my year in Brussels was drawing to a close, a presentiment of melancholy established itself within me. The presentiment took me by surprise; I had after all chosen the most ungrateful destination in Europe – the Eurocrat valley with its fairies and brownies. I had even called them plasticised. Towards the end I caught myself booking one cheap flight after the other far into the year 2010, with the direction – plasticisers. I conjoined a vision with these flights. I wanted to go on holiday in Brussels. Holiday in the European institutions.

I imagined arriving in the morning. The Métro sets me in motion right away. I feel like I'm in a video clip; pop or classical music resounding through the stations, African beauties underlining the exoticism of my destination.

Having breakfast in the European Commission. In order to feel at ease, I arrive in the fitting leisurely fashion; suit and tie, cuff links are donned. I grab the press review of the day and sit down in the least stimulating cafeteria of the confederation. In the hundred page haystack that is the press review I look for the pin of a Commission-critical report, however don't get annoyed at all but simply dunk my cheap Commission croissant in my just as cheap Commission coffee.

Afterwards, a conference with a lunch buffet would come just at the right time. With pleasure, I let myself be lulled for a while. "Civil society", "best practice", "communicate sustainable consumption", are what the Europeans need right now. The best recreation value would be offered by a conference like the lobby that I visited at the time mainly because of its name: "Chemical Regions". I was the first one at the buffet, I went back for seconds twice. Then we were called for the press briefing.

A German was sitting upfront, visibly wired after the arrival of the Commissioner of Enterprise and Industry; next to me were two journalists. The journalists were posing competent questions, seemingly about the integration of the European chemical regions. I had no clue, no question; I started to feel embarrassed. In order to also have said something I posed a general question according to Brusselian fashion: "Do you see yourself as a civil servant or a politician?" The wired German stared at me in shock. "Er, as a politician. I'm the Finance Minster of Saxony-Anhalt."

As my destination for the afternoon I will definitely choose the European Parliament. I would never take the holiday plane when the EP meets in Strasbourg. I hang out for a while in the bright open space of the Mickey

Mouse bar, overlooking the park outside and the female interns inside. I have a cheap "lait russe", later a just as cheap glass of port wine, "un euro nonante".

My holiday happiness is completed with a six-thirty-reception. Either someone gives me a tip or I haphazardly wander through the rooms leading up to the "Members' Restaurant". Like back in the days, when I paced around the ladies at the reception with natural grace and found myself at the purely British reception of the purely British "Food and Drink Federation". The door to the small room was closed; I was the only one without a nametag on my lapel. The caviar biscuits were exquisite. Too late did I notice that to every delegate, assistant or journalist there was one flown-in female English lobbyist. "Are you interested in food?" I heard suddenly. I looked down and saw a little lady with thin lips smiling vaguely, "Food and Drink Federation" was written on her tag. She meant me. I swallowed hard.

Later during the six-thirty-reception Staszek joins me, without my heartbroken mate the holiday is worthless. Hunger satisfied and moderately pre-heated, we stick to the old habits of my active days; we head towards the Africans. Isn't that the most important thing, what really enriched me in my Eurocrat-year; this new desire for Africa? This time I'm going for the full monty. At least once I will have chips, and when hunger plagues me in the middle of the night, I'll have a bowl of hot soup with the unwinding transsexual prostitutes from Alhambra. I won't set any meetings, I won't book a hotel, in an emergency there is always a room available in my trusted hotel by the hour. That's life. That's how I imagine a holiday.

"And what are you doing in Brussels?" casual acquaintances will ask me, whose time slots I accidently cross, the briefers and briefees of the working capital of Europe. "I'm on holiday", I will reply with a firm voice, "I'm on holiday in the European institutions." The facial expressions that I will be rewarded with this phrase will be my greatest leisure.

Final Remark

Once, when I was young and depressed, I unexpectedly made a group of young Austrian women dream. I described to the young ladies how an attractive European empirical couple travelled through Europe in a palace car, and received glowing looks in return. If need be, Eurovisionary could also be a profession, I thought, but didn't follow through with this career.

After my return I sorted out what I could have learned during my year in Brussels. Altogether, I had gone through twenty-seven sleeping places. Not because of the twenty-seven Member States, twenty-seven was a coincidence. Every week I wrote one story. I didn't write about bittersweet chocolate or about Belgian chocolate beer. I wandered through a valley in which almost everything is political. Nevertheless, I barely wrote anything about politics, European politics is almost always too extensive for a column. Many things I still don't understand, many things I don't want to understand. However, I do know a little something.

Surely, I didn't go to Brussels to once in my life see people dream about the institutions of the European Union. I couldn't expect that in this centre of administration, at eye level with enterprise, enterprise is what you see. Admittedly, I went wherever the word "vision" was mentioned, for example once, to a series of talks by the leading think-tank "European Policy Centre", where the young and active of the European bubble could recite their European visions. On the evening I was listening, all participants were supposed to have prepared a vision of how to overcome the financial crisis. Halfway through I ran out filled with consternation. Four, five participants after another had presented an identical solution to the crisis – additional paid trial years within the European Commission.

After my return I tally up the times I had experienced debates about the shape of Europe in the Eurocrat valley. Some discussions come back to me. I tally up again and rub my eyes. I notice that I had indeed discussed the topic of the institutional shape of Europe with Staszek, Liliana and many others, but that I was always the one raising the topic. The thing is, and hereby I already reveal the main finding of my expeditions in the capital: there is nothing more to say about Europe.

In 2009 I was invited to a big international conference in the Viennese Hofburg Palace. The occasion was the twentieth anniversary of the fall of the Iron Curtain. It was a grand ballroom filled with politicians, diplomats, dignitaries, audience. On the podium, central European students were supposed to discuss with central European writers. About visions for the future of Europe. Once again, I was right.

First of all, the three writers were supposed to tell of their memories of 1989. So we did, a Czech, a Slovak and me. In truth, I didn't have anything to say. I was seventeen in 1989, there was no revolution in Lower Austria. I therefore told of how I became a head boy in my convent school in 1989 and had to fight for a coke machine. Personally, I didn't want a coke machine, but my voters did. As a result I withdrew from politics. The audience laughed.

Next were the European visions of the students. In fact, the Polish student couldn't separate the Lisbon Strategy from the Lisbon Treaty, yet all students complied with the on such occasions emerging type of the appointed nerd. The boredom fell upon me like manna from heaven. The moderator tried to steer in the other direction, posed pointed questions to the students, who however hadn't elaborated further on their thoughts than their prepared statements. They only repeated how positive they found the many opportunities offered in a united Europe. They were right.

The elections to the European Parliament were approaching. The moderator asked everyone on the podium whether they were going to vote. They all said yes. It was mentioned that the EU had to provide better information about itself. I was last in line. I replied that I had just come from Brussels and that my answer would therefore be extensive and that I would therefore like to pass. The moderator probed persistently. I let myself be persuaded to share a future vision and said something down the lines of: "You could make a democracy out of the EU."

I hadn't believed this point of view to be scandalous. The next moment I felt like a ruffian who was buggering up the hosts' party. The dignitaries sat frozen in their seats. The organisers were appalled. A minority, maybe a quarter of the audience in the room, started to applaud vigorously. Alois Mock was sitting on first row, the Austrian Minister of Foreign Affairs in 1989, a graduate from the same convent school as I. The seriously ill man looked irritated. I felt ashamed. The moderator left me out during the next round of questions. An official from the "Pan-European Movement" stood up from the audience and called my vision "cheap". I thought to myself, now what have I done, they'll never invite me back, luckily mum hadn't been watching!

As I was leaving the Hofburg, several young women spoke to me in the entrance hall. I hadn't made the girls within the Ministry of Foreign Affairs dream, but they grinned at me with thievish pleasure. They congratulated me, I think to my bravery. They were actually good-looking. Eurodissident would also be a profession, if need be, I thought befuddled. However, Václav Klaus was already filling that position.

The Nationalists, who again and again were elected into the European Parliament, didn't interest me at all. To me they are a cog in the wheel. Without effort they profit from the elitist, abstract, regulating cipher which the poor, mangy, dingy city of Brussels became in the eyes of the rest of Europe. Isn't it striking that, amongst all the emerging and descending right-wing populists, barely anyone demanded for their country to leave the EU? If Brussels hadn't already been built, these people would have invented it.

It was the Czech President who explicitly called himself a dissident of the EU. Towards the end, Václav Klaus exchanged his signature on the Lisbon Treaty for a cementation of the Beneš decrees, the basis on which seven million Czechs had robbed and expelled three million Sudeten Germans. I don't applaud this political dealing. I was however inspired by his essay called "What is Europeism?" In the essay, Klaus describes "Europeism" as a "metaideology" "of different post-democratic-isms". I now go forth and steal that expression from Klaus. What Klaus mentioned as the contents of Europeism can only have been a small introduction. His list was lopsided; it wasn't complete.

After my return from the alignments of offices and the living environments of the Europeists I made my own list. Europeism, as I see it, contains the following: corporatism, consensualism, multilateralism, competitism, evaluism, genderism, NGOism, advisorism, stakeholderism, gremialism, say-civil-society-instead-of-lobby-ism, consultantism, elitism, hygienism, eat-no-fat-ism, don't-smoke-ism, ecologism, take-one-napkin-instead-of-two-ism, climatism, controlism, resume-fanatism, rationalism, liberalism, homosexualism, secularism, anticatholicism, briefingism, harmonism, security-fetishism, pavement-rectificationism, internet-exclusivism, facebookism, assessmentism, awareness-rise-ism, correctism, adult-education-rigidism, lifestyle-statism, the-superior-bullshitism.

After my return, I ponder over the open questions. Where does it all lead? Who wanted it this way? How could it have gone this far? If there had been one, I would have read a historical analysis about this with trembling hands; how the central culture had emerged, which trickling and creeping had made an impact on the rest of Europe. The Eurocrats are indeed good, but they're not the best. Were the Eurocrats the best, they would set stages on fire or govern global corporations. Their ultimate weapon is the boredom they spread.

I would really like to know where they come from, the ingredients for the real existing Europeism. The culture of short and concentrated briefings remind me of America, from where the fascinated Soviet travellers Ilf and Petrov already reported in 1936: "No one is kept waiting for an 'appointment', because the time is usually fixed with absolute precision and the conversation does not take a single extra minute." France comes to mind when observing the state of the Brusselian civil servants, the state of highly appreciated and privileged civil servant nobility of well-tempered rationality, which is incomprehensible to many Member States.

Further then, Germany. According to popular opinion, only the constant modesty of the strongest nation enabled the advancing European integration. There's a great deal of truth to that; Germany renounced the D-Mark, voting rights, executive positions. The price that Europe pays for Germany's generosity seems high to me though. The German corporatism was implemented on the level of the European communities. Imagine this, in sixty years of European integration the greatest nation of the confederation was never polled about Europe. The vague proposal of a referendum alone triggers indignant disgust amongst the federal republic's opinion leadership: how could we let something as important as Europe be decided by the mood of the voters?

The "no alternative" mainstream of German European politics, the broad maelstrom of what the Christian Democrats, the Social Democrats, the Liberals and the Greens would never question, advances in even more broad and winding ways in Brussels. The concepts of government and opposition get lost indefinitely in the thousand-finger co-ruling-structure of Brussels' Eurocrat valley. Always, everyone's responsible, or no one. The contest of voters choosing a policy or dropping it has been nullified. European politics equals the dissolution of politics. The actual political matter, determined by committees, is settled without dispute. Afterwards the citizen is informed, things are communicated, some are explained.

But what am I talking about, talking about the shape of Europe has ceased. In 1984, the European Parliament decided on the first outline of a European constitution, in 2001 the European Convention was established, finally in 2009 the Lisbon Treaty came into effect. According to the preamble, the aim of the Treaty was "to complete the process […] enhancing the efficiency and democratic legitimacy of the Union".

It took twenty-five years of retching in order to finish a Europe that is administrated by many more unelected liaison offices than ever before. A Europe, which calls for more Presidents than ever before. It calls for a President of the European Commission, a President of the European Parliament, a permanent President of the European Council, a Minister of Foreign Affairs presiding a High Representative and a Vice President of the Commission, it calls for biannually rotating Presidents of the Council of the European Union. The heads of states of the rotating presidency also want to preside.

The first permanent President of the European Council was a geezer from Flanders, thanks very much for that. After all this retching no one will want to talk about another shape of Europe, for a long time. With a bit of bad luck, the European machine will conduct us to the end of our days. Eurorealist could also be a profession, I thought rationally. The most rational though, would be getting a job within the eternally established European institutions. Not to save my life, never.

I'm not completely young anymore and not at all depressed, my wanderings through the east, the centre and occasionally also the west of Europe make me exceedingly happy. At times I cursed myself for having chosen the Valley of the Eurocrats of all places as the destination of my forays. I obviously have a defect, an urge, a repulsive streak. There's nothing else to say about Europe, however

I want to continue talking. I want to continue talking, at table and bedsides, tipsy and sober, by day and by night. No one will want to talk to me, talking about Europe has ceased. Again, all that remains is flight. So I escape into a frivolous game.

Sex and the Valley

Once again, I'm standing at the Brusselian meat market, in place Lux. A small old-town square, made ready for winter with heat lamps and small plastic roofs. Hundreds of young European professionals all squeezed together. Once more I ask myself if a piece of TV-entertainment couldn't be carved out of these good-looking people. If the Valley of the Eurocrats wouldn't be a good setting for a TV-series after all. I would call it "Sex and the Valley", based on the series from New York.

Ladies and gentlemen of Europe's TV-broadcasters, I look about me here in place Lux. Dressed-up people, mostly in their initiative Brusselian period, yet every single one is already representing the interests of tens of thousands of people somewhere. They're from all European countries, but many reply in English even when addressed in their mother tongue. The TV-audience will most certainly hate these little whippersnappers.

That's good, that's very good. Isn't the TV-audience attracted to elitist, unattainable and unlikable settings?

Who likes rich kids from Beverly Hills or oil barons from Dallas and who doesn't watch the series set in those environments? Isn't the place Lux the perfect location, where a normal person instantly wins our hearts?

I contemplate whether I know any fitting characters in Brussels for the series. At least one absolutely normal guy comes to mind. A small civil servant, one last Mohican from the family altar that is Poland. Solid, decent, with a small roundish belly that shows through his old-fashioned stripy shirts. Ever since the enlargement to the east, he hasn't been able to find a girlfriend. He suffers like a dog in place Lux. The audience suffers with him, enduring every one of his rendezvous.

As female counterpart I'm thinking about a small Italian. She loves eating and toils for a small mocked sector lobby: the Maize Millers. She is single, however doesn't go to place Lux, she doesn't want any of these men. She loves smells and considers Brussels to be completely devoid of them. I think that she's not particularly romantic. Men don't matter to her very much. She wants a child though. That might work out. The Maize Miller and the Last of the Mohicans, they don't know each other. How are they supposed to find each other?

Ladies and gentlemen, when choosing evil supporting characters I have a number of options. I think of a lift lobbyist, who speaks wide-eyed about crushed cleaning ladies and grandmothers left lying on stairs. With this he wants to secure orders for modifications for his lift industry. I think of a tobacco lobbyist who purrs out of pure lust for life and works for well-run private clinics in order to round off his portfolio. However, before all of them I think of the elite of the elite, of the graduates from the College of Europe in Bruges. They all end up in Brussels, some as think-tank tank-thinkers; they're insuperable. If they're spotted, the mere mortal Eurocrats mumble amongst themselves with a grudging prolongation of the English pronunciation of Bruges: "Brrooosh".

From the middle of the Brrooosh nobility, the most popular lobbyist for hire in the Eurocrat valley sticks out. Gold-blond hair, hazelnut doe eyes, perfect mastery of comitology. She has to be one of the main characters; her nationality really doesn't matter. She's involved in helping mutilated African children, and all the more convincing she charms for the filthiest businesses in the world. She can blush on command. She doesn't seem cold at all.

The Brrooosh-bird cannot be conquered. At most, she would find one guy acceptable, a cartel hunter for the Commission. This guy actually washes his hands before every handshake, but he brings action to our programme. We see him sitting in a nameless hotel in the single market, with other dashing guys. Plotting like field marshals, the cartel hunters sit bent over *Google maps* planning their dawn raids.

Later, we see an electric torch roving through the deep of the night. A delinquent is, without authorisation, breaking the seal of the European Commission. There's a scare, the Commission seal is suddenly ranging in all colours, it's a very up-to-date seal. Suddenly, a word appears on the seal: "void". Even in the dark, we detect that the seal breaker turns pale.

The Brrooosh-bird is friends with the Maize Miller, and the lonesome Mohican has a mate too. His mate is a columnist. He started his Brusselian column according to the measure: "Give us this day our daily bendy cucumbers!" The readers abandoned him; since then he writes more spiced-up stories, tries to establish himself as a kind of Carrie Bradshaw in the European capital. His mostly snappy and rarely affectionate columns are about the meat market in the Valley of the Eurocrats. That gives a framework to the story line. Devoted, the columnist compares the up-to-date phraseology of the briefings with the filth of the resentments within Europe. "Safeguard future economic and social well-being", we hear the long-serving western European Commission aunties tooting smoothly. When the new eastern European colleague leaves for her lunch meeting, the tone is slightly modified: "What a slut, probably slept her way to the top, did'ya see those nails, how cheap!"

Our columnist is different from Carrie Bradshaw; he's a broken bastard. Without even having gone one square kilometre outside of Brussels, he shags his way through the most unlikely regions of Europe. This character, ladies and gentlemen, is expressly not portraying the author of this book himself. He's not me. He's a fictitious columnist who together with an unhappy Mohican goes out in hot pursuit.

You would think that no one lets themselves get involved with the cynical gossip journalist. Still, in every episode he has a new one in his arm; not only naive interns. He's crazy about one girl, this one he would more than any want to conquer. She's the Brrooosh-bird, who despises him, but she engages herself in the most ludicrous cross talks with the columnist swine. Isn't there a big, soft heart, disappointed by the European reality, beating under his unbearable exterior? Wouldn't he stay, if she would have him, blissfully with the bird from Brrooosh? Would the beast of a lobbyist for hire turn out to be the fairy most capable of love in the whole Eurocrat valley?

In the end we go back to place Lux, again and again. The Last of the Mohicans, sad and introverted, is quietly shaking his head. The Maize Miller is sitting in her germfree office and melancholically smelling white corn. The corn doesn't smell like anything anymore. I agree, ladies and gentlemen, that you call "Sex and the Valley" a frivolous game, a game involving for a long time the unchangeable conditions of the European Union. If Europe doesn't come to a good end, then at least the series should. It has to.